ZEN AND HAPPINESS

ZEN AND HAPPINESS

Practical Insights and Meditations to Cultivate Joy in Everyday Life

JOSHUA R. PASZKIEWICZ

ROCKRIDGE
PRESS

First Rockridge Press paperback edition June 2022

Rockridge Press and the Rockridge Press logo are trademarks or registered trademarks of Callisto Media Inc. and/or its affiliates in the United States and other countries and may not be used without written permission.

For general information on our other products and services, please contact our Customer Care Department within the United States at (866) 744-2665, or outside the United States at (510) 253-0500.

Paperback ISBN: 978-1-63878-478-4 | eBook ISBN: 978-1-63878-658-0

Manufactured in the United States of America

Interior and Cover Designer: Brieanna H. Felschow
Art Producer: Sara Feinstein
Editor: Carolyn Abate
Production Editor: Rachel Taenzler
Production Manager: Martin Worthington

0 1 2 3 4 5 6 7 8 9 10

CHAPTER 1

A BRIEF HISTORY OF ZEN

Establishing a Zen practice can be a simple task, but it's certainly not a small one. So in this chapter, we'll prepare by examining the history, development, and varied expressions of the Zen tradition. We'll touch on numerous points of foundational philosophy to orient you to Zen's varied meditative and inquisitive processes. You'll be introduced to basic concepts to help ready and center you so you can get the most out of your Zen journey.

WHAT IS ZEN?

Strictly speaking, *zen* is a Japanese word derived from the Chinese word *chan*, which in turn is rendered from the Sanskrit word *dhyana*. Each of these terms essentially means "meditation" or "contemplation." Originally, the words were rather generic descriptors of an array of silent and seated introspective practices common to religions of the Indian subcontinent. But around 520 CE, with the arrival in China of a semi-mythic Indian Buddhist sage named Bodhidharma, Zen began to take on special significance. Bodhidharma is widely considered to be the progenitor of the Zen tradition. His core teaching was that Zen is "a special transmission outside of the scriptures, that is not dependent on words or letters, but which directly points toward the true nature of mind, allowing one to become awakened."

As an evolving spiritual tradition, Zen exists as a continual stream of individualized instruction, passed on from teacher to student, rather than as a mere collection of doctrines and orthodoxies. Zen is not a path of cultivating morality or virtue particularly, nor worshipping a guru or deity. Instead, Zen is a method of holistically and meticulously examining your own life and overcoming the commonly garnered inaccurate, and often inadequate, conceptions of how life works.

It's fair to say Zen is a philosophy and practice that's deeply rooted in the foundational teachings of Siddhartha Gautama, the fifth-century religious teacher commonly known throughout the world as the Buddha. What sets Zen apart from other schools of Buddhist thought and practice is that Zen is meant to be a current, living expression of the Buddha's awakening, as opposed to a mere transmission of his teachings. This makes it hard to define Zen, as it's always adapting to current circumstances and presenting itself differently to each individual seeking its wisdom.

The "awakening" that Zen proposes isn't some supernatural, otherworldly, metaphysical phenomenon. What we're talking about is developing an intimate awareness of the very marrow of life itself, derived from the insights gained through the practice of concentrated attention. Zen is concerned absolutely with the contents of your life and experience. Zen seeks to cut through our misconceptions of reality and invites us into the freedom and joy that come with freeing ourselves from conventional, delusional—and usually unconsciously inherited—patterns of stifled thinking.

How do we get there? Zen challenges us to examine—perhaps for the very first time—all that we know and believe to be true. Leaving no stone unturned, the Zen adept learns to find refuge in that which can be known—and since mysteries can only be intuited and inferred, to abide comfortably in the unknowing. It is only in this place, says Zen, that lasting peace, joy, and true happiness can be known.

MISCONCEPTIONS OF ZEN

Did you pick up this book thinking you had some knowledge of what Zen is all about, but now you're not so sure? That's understandable. Zen is a frequently misappropriated concept. The word *Zen* conjures up all sorts of images for the average person, from a kind of semi-spiritual simplicity to advertisements for sleek, modern products and experiences ranging from e-cigarettes to nightclubs. While the term *Zen* is often conflated with popular notions of minimalism and simplicity, the heart of the tradition is beyond such oversimplifications, which serve to obscure the actual living practice that is Zen.

On one end of the of Zen misconception spectrum, the tradition is sometimes billed as an exclusionary religious practice that's mired in premodern Buddhist religiosity. At the other extreme, it's been deemed a philosophy of life, steeped in the smoke of antiestablishment sentiments that defined the so-called Beat Generation of the 1950s and '60s. Parts of the Zen tradition can be found in both those descriptions. But any exclusive characterization therefrom tends to miss the reality that only the actual practice and study of Zen can reveal.

Let's take a closer look at some popular myths about Zen.

Myth: Zen is undefinable.

Truth: The reality is, Zen does have plainly discernible boundaries. Though not finite, Zen's bounds are continually refined by the times and cultures in which Zen finds itself planted.

Myth: Practicing Zen means becoming a Buddhist.

Truth: As we've noted, Zen is broadly situated within the Buddhist tradition, and thanks to these roots it employs Buddhist imagery and language in its practice. However, Zen is not a spiritual practice that revolves around any notion of a creating or controlling god or gods. Theists, atheists, and nontheists alike are all free to explore the practice of Zen. It should also be noted that Zen isn't a practice limited to monks or priests. Almost from its beginnings, the practice of Zen has been enjoyed by both full-time monastic practitioners and laypeople alike. Zen is not limited by the scriptures of the Buddhist canon, either, or those of any other religion or philosophy. The Zen tradition can be found in many writings. Chief among them are the collections of dialogues between Zen teachers and their students, which we call koan anthologies.

Myth: Zen is a form of meditation.

Truth: The discipline of a seated meditation practice is universal to all schools of Zen. But the tradition is not tied to the meditation cushion. Rather, the central and most universal discipline of Zen is the mutual tending to an ongoing mentored relationship between a student and a teacher.

Myth: Zen is supposed to be difficult.

Truth: While practicing Zen has a reputation for being somewhat rigorous, and even harsh at times, it need not be so to be effective. What the practice of Zen does require is a meaningful commitment developed and sustained over time. But Zen can be practiced successfully in a relatively gentle and relaxed manner, and advanced Zen practice assuredly is.

THE FOUR NOBLE TRUTHS

Because Zen has its roots in Buddhism, it's important for practitioners to understand the core teachings of Buddhist tradition.

Buddhism tells us that Siddhartha Gautama, who would become known as the Buddha, was born into a noble family, with access to all of the wealth and privileges available during his time. But Gautama was struck by the realities of old age, sickness, and death—the temporal nature of human life. He asked, how can humans be happy knowing that we are to die, despite all of our attempts at achieving well-being? It was this inquiry that propelled Gautama's own search for answers, for meaning, and for freedom from a preoccupation with knowing.

The Buddha's initial teaching effort resulted in the Four Noble Truths: dukkha, samudaya, nirodha, and marga. In simple terms, these four words are translated into suffering, the cause of suffering, the end of suffering, and the path. Think of them as a statement of the problem, its analysis, the solution, and its enactment. The Four Noble Truths, especially dukkha and samudaya, don't seek to explain precisely *why* suffering exists. The Zen teaching on suffering is concerned with *how* it exists.

The Zen path is for people prepared to transcend theorizing and storytelling, to get to work on the things that can be known and that can be worked on in our lives.

Suffering

The first concept that comprises the teaching of the Four Noble Truths is dukkha. It's a Sanskrit word that means "a wheel that binds," but that is often colloquially understood as "suffering." Simply put, the Zen tradition begins with the realization that suffering exists, in ways big and small. The fundamental nature of the human condition—regardless of how we got this way—is tinged with disappointment. But if not why, then perhaps more important, we might ask, how?

The Cause of Suffering

The second Noble Truth is samudaya, another Sanskrit word that essentially references the causes and conditions of this wheel-sticking suffering (or dukkha). In other words, "how?" Zen notes that this dissatisfaction, which is common to human experience, typically arises when we regard and treat the impermanent, temporal, and transitory things in our lives as if they were anything else. When we cling and attach to things that cannot be successfully clung or attached to, we give rise to craving and desiring things to be other than they are. In short, we become infatuated with impossibility because we perceive things to be in ways other than they really are, and in this we suffer.

The End of Suffering

Sans a narrative storyline, the first two assertions can seem bleak in their outlook. Some have miscast Buddhism at large as a religion of nihilism because of this. But the Zen teaching on suffering is concerned with *how* it exists as a way of finding a solution. The Zen path is for people prepared to transcend theorizing and storytelling, to get to work on the things that can be known and that can be worked on. Enter, then, the third Noble Truth, nirodha, or cessation. This asserts that things don't have to be this way. We can find ourselves on the other side of our suffering and transcend its grip on our experience.

The Path

Remember, Zen is concerned with "not why, but how." And the "how" is the fourth Noble Truth, or marga, the path forward. It's known better to the body of foundational Zen teachings as the Eightfold Path, consisting of right view, right intention, right speech, right action, right livelihood, right effort, right mindfulness, and right concentration. These eight aspects, which we'll examine more closely, are to be developed in tandem, as each supports the others. Together, they promote the essential elements of Buddhist practice: ethical conduct, mental stewardship, and the cultivation of wisdom. Specific to Zen, the use of "right" is more like the righting of a vessel that's veering off course. In a very real sense, from the Zen perspective, what is "right" is defined only by what is happening *right now*, in this very moment, as there is no alternative reality to flee to. What is right is simply what is now, and things simply are as they are. It is in viewing them as such that we can come to accept them and thereby respond to reality itself in accordance with reality as it is. Immediately, then, we suffer less.

THE EIGHTFOLD PATH

Right view: The Buddha teaches that the way to find ourselves on the other side of our suffering is to see things as they *are*, rather than as they are not. The way to do this is to cultivate right view. Generally speaking, the Zen interpretation of the fourth Noble Truth of marga (or the path leading toward the cessation of suffering) is entirely contained within the notion of right view. As you may recall, the very word *Zen* means concentrated meditative awareness—seeing things just as they are. The hope is that an awareness of reality as it is will facilitate an acceptance of reality as it is, which then affords accord with reality as it is and, ultimately, harmony with reality in our intentions; in our speech; in our actions and in the ways we make a living; in our efforts at cultivating happiness, joy, and liberation; in the ways that we show up in the present moment; and in our attempts at investing ourselves fully in that moment.

Right intention: When setting foot to the path of Zen, it is important to take a survey of our intention and resolve. The path of awakening is not to be traversed lightly or recreationally. Any intention other than one tending toward a holistic, radical reorientation to one's life and way of being will likely set one's foray into the path of Zen up for failure. While in a very real sense, the right intention is the one we can muster in any given moment, the intention that will carry us through on our endeavor to become awake and aware people may be something to proactively tend to and grow to appropriate proportions.

Right speech: Our speech includes not only the things we say but the words and conceptions we think. Our conceptual (and often habitual) thought significantly colors our world and defines our experience, and thereby our well-being (or lack thereof). The Zen cultivar must pay close mind to their words and concepts, as the lifelong practice of putting them to work in forging our reality will likely pale our efforts of mindful realization if not stewarded with care.

Right action: Right action is any action defined by awareness and intentionality, which are in many ways the first fruits of Zen practice and ideally informed by the sense of agency that our practice refines. Our conduct is a chief contributor to the strings of causality and effect known to the Zen Buddhist tradition of karma-vipaka, which can then ripple far into our future and move our experience toward awakening and well-being or away from it with equal ease.

Right livelihood: Our livelihood is in essence the means by which we make our lives, certainly in a financial sense (with its plentiful karmic implications) but also in a sense of our choices ultimately serving to sculpt our experience. If we make choices in accord with the wisdom born of our practice, our lives will reflect it and, despite any ease or difficulty encountered, ultimately be definable appropriately as "right."

Right effort: In accord with an understanding of causality and effect (karma-vipaka), it is easily noted that our efforts will be met with results of like kind, so long as they are possible amid the grander (even cosmic) forces already at work in our lives. We should not expect to practice little, or merely intellectually surmise awakened living, and expect to actually undergo a transformation toward the authentic and sustainable happiness known to awakened people.

Right mindfulness: In the sense of the Eightfold Path, right mindfulness is essentially concerned with how we show up in any given moment, with the amount of due attention that we pay to our lived experience (rather than to mere cognitive overlays or daydreams). Our lives happen right here and right now, always. Stewarding a sense of intentional awareness, of actual concentrated attention in all times and places, is the only way to realize awakening and liberation.

Right concentration: Right concentration may also be translated as right absorption, or right union with our experience. This notion pertains, then, to the potential investing of ourselves fully in the moment as integrated beings. In this, right concentration is non-different from awakening itself and therefore the field of experience that gives rise to happiness in every situation where happiness is in appropriate accord with reality, and therefore possible.

HOW ZEN DIFFERS FROM OTHER TRADITIONS

As a whole, the Buddhist tradition is somewhere around 2,600 years old. Orthodox Buddhism, known as Theravada Buddhism ("the way of the elders"), seeks to preserve the original teachings of the Buddha as closely as possible. Over time, however, circumstances resulted in a reformation to the orthodox school that became known broadly as the Mahayana ("great vehicle") school. As the Buddhist tradition found its reach extending far beyond its culture of origin, revisitations of its fundamental doctrines sometimes resulted in unrecognizable and entirely new forms of practice. As these began to encounter other religious and spiritual schools, syncretism began to take hold, resulting in hybrid traditions mixing Buddhist orthodoxy and indigenous, non-Buddhist spirituality, the most famous example of which we today call Vajrayana ("diamond vehicle" or "thunderbolt vehicle").

In the face of an assortment of rigid orthodoxy, new and unrecognizable reformation traditions, and often-confusing hybrids, restoration movements sought to recapture the original nature of the Buddha. Here we encounter Zen. It's a tradition that incorporates the foundational suppositions of Buddhist orthodoxy, the keen critical insights of the Buddhist reformation traditions, and the wisdom of Buddhism meeting the wider world. Zen reduces all these influences to their common functional units, resulting in an earthy, raw, and living school of thought and practice.

Zen does not require belief as it is commonly understood nor the religiosity and metaphysics that are found in its parent and competing Buddhist traditions. Zen retains no premodern notions of biology and cosmology found in Buddhist orthodoxy, for example. And the tradition has criticized the religiosity and unsubstantiated metaphysics of Mahayana Buddhism, and certainly has shed the shamanistic roots and concerns for literal magic found in some other traditions such as Vajrayana. That said, what Zen has retained and integrated is a profound sense of skillful means (known in Buddhism as upaya). When deemed helpful, Zen has freely co-opted practices from other Buddhist schools and employed them toward the aims and objectives of the Zen tradition itself—namely, the full awakening of its adherents, in this very lifetime, as liberated, aware, and fully human, happy beings.

Zen, in its simplest form, requires only that people show up and try. In fact, the most classical instruction for the basics of entering the Zen way is simply, and perhaps a bit crassly, to "sit down, shut up, and pay attention."

THE BENEFITS OF ZEN

A traditional Zen trope offers that Zen is "good for nothing." This speaks to Zen's embrace of our lives as they are, rather than of any otherworldly dream state. The Zen tradition doesn't seek to transform us into anything other than what we are; it doesn't seek to deliver us to any place other than this moment. What the practice of Zen is based upon is the simple notion that somehow, if we strip down to the essentials of bare awareness, our present experience—now and always—is enough. And happiness takes care of itself, if we let it.

The benefits of Zen, if there are indeed benefits to be had from a good-for-nothing practice, are that we wake up to what has always been true to our experience. In other words, the benefits of Zen are the benefits of living life in its fullness and being in touch with that life, rather than being lost in some conceptualization about it. Through practicing the concentrated awareness that comprises the discipline of Zen, we become able to let what is be what is.

We can find freedom from the need to control every detail. To find enough, to have enough, to be enough— that is what Zen offers.

SITTING MEDITATION

For many, the word *Zen* is synonymous with seated meditation, also commonly known as zazen. The discipline of actually sitting down, quieting down, and paying attention can be particularly profound. Here is where we are most likely to meet ourselves, to be confronted by the barrage of thought streams that comprise our consciousness. When we're "on the seat," we often learn how little control we have over the musings of our minds, how little insight we have into the mind's contents, and even how inadequate our present self-concepts are.

At times in meditation we may find ourselves preoccupied with a particular aspect of meditative inquiry, and at times we may find our practice to simply be one of nurturing broad awareness. In short, everything that happens on the seat is correct, so long as we keep returning to it and, when possible, keep checking in with a competent Zen teacher or meditative guide.

While the specifics of beginning and maintaining a Zen meditation practice will be explored in this book, it's important here to note that "to sit" in Zen meditation is both a physical practice and a mental posture or orientation. Without a doubt, sitting Zen is a core practice of Zen that should be tended to on a regular basis, and it's not something you graduate from. However, with time and constancy, the process of sitting can become so integrated into our psyche that it can be difficult to separate the practice on the seat from the state of mind we carry throughout the whole of our life and experience. It's wise to not bring goals into the practice of sitting meditation.

But it's useful to always move in a direction of, and with an aspiration toward, integrating the practice with the rest of your life and the routine demands of daily life.

To practice Zen in all forms is to practice awareness, to steward awareness, and to otherwise concentrate awareness into the presence that enlivens our bodies. In living our lives in both mundane and grand moments, we might come to anchor ourselves to the current moment, and this moment then to us. And with that, the stillness that so many of us seek is made manifest. This is the psychic orientation of sitting, which is a significant marker of integration but never the goal.

An important point about goals: A spiritual practice that entertains *goals* idealizes attaining them, and this effectively blinds you from the ongoing experience of the journey of life. On the spiritual path, *aspirations* are a natural and even healthy response to the tendency to form goals. But distinction between the two should be made.

KARMA: MORE THAN WHAT GOES AROUND COMES AROUND

Karma is one of those terms that gets thrown around a lot but is seldom understood. In relation to the practice of Zen, karma is to be understood not as a cosmic record of merits and demerits but rather as a natural law of cause and effect. Indeed, the word *karma* is actually but one half of a compounded term, *karma-vipaka*, which means "the ripening of causes or actions." Understanding and tending to karma-vipaka in real time is an essential process for our Zen practice. We mustn't mistake the pragmatic law of karma-vipaka for an amorphous, quasi-metaphysical dogma that pawns off personal responsibility.

When we pay mind to the consequences of our actions (and inactions) as well as to the causes and conditions we encounter in life by no conscious choice of our own, we shift our mode of being from impulsive reactivity to intentional responsiveness. That is, we begin to respond instead of react. Responses arise from a combination of awareness and intention, whereas reactions are habits, frequently unexamined, which were conditioned into us rather than cultivated by us.

KEY TAKEAWAYS

- Zen arose from the Buddhist tradition around 520 CE, with the arrival of the sage Bodhidharma in China.

- Zen is deeply rooted in the foundational teachings of Buddhism, the Four Noble Truths, and the Eightfold Path. Zen seeks to produce awakened beings in the here and now, rather than to transmit orthodox teachings or scriptures that rely on the accumulation of merit for eventual personal deliverance from suffering.

- Zen teaches us to meticulously examine our own life and overcome inaccurate conceptions of how life works so we can find refuge in that which can be known and otherwise abide comfortably in unknowing. It is only in this place that lasting peace, joy, and true happiness can be known.

- Some myths about Zen include: It requires becoming a Buddhist (it doesn't); Zen is simply a form of meditation (it's not, though meditation does play a substantial role); Zen is meant to be difficult to practice (Zen can be practiced gently).

CHAPTER 2

BUILDING A ZEN PRACTICE FOR HAPPINESS

In this chapter, we will begin to move beyond examining the history, development, and foundational philosophy of the Zen tradition and enter into the work of building a practice. In the coming pages, we will work to define happiness so as to clarify a direction for our practice and examine the practical concept of the "beginner's mind" while exploring Zen's relationship to the contemporary mindfulness movement, before finally receiving instruction on the basics of Zen meditation and koan practice.

DEFINING HAPPINESS

Happiness is a somewhat elusive concept. It's an abstract notion that human beings all seem to universally prize and search for but that few of us can clearly define. In modern culture happiness if often considered to be something of a moving target, expanding and changing as soon we get close to it. We think, *If only I had ____, then I would be happy.* But as soon as we get that thing, we become dissatisfied and move on to the next "if only." Cultivating happiness through the practice of Zen depends upon conceiving of happiness in a realistic and meaningful way, beyond the endless craving of more and more of every good thing. Happiness is less a finite state of being than it is a process and an orientation to the whole of your life and experience.

That said, there is no doubt that much of the time, for many of us, happiness is centered around a state of being or a particular experience. However, as Zen Buddhist teaching points out, impermanence always applies. That's just reality, and it won't yield much to our attempts at molding it into anything else. So Buddhism as a whole and Zen in particular aren't much concerned with attaining and maintaining this impermanent state. Rather, the task at hand for the Zen discipline is liberation from the suffering that arises in attempting to make the impermanent permanent. That freedom allows us to go anywhere that our experience takes us, without being overcome by wistfulness for things to be any way other than they are. To no small degree, that is the nature of awakening that Zen practitioners aspire to. And it's not a coincidence that throughout history the awakened people and teachers among us have been typically perceived as happy, despite often simultaneously displaying a profound capacity for tending to sorrow and heartbreak.

True happiness is a process, not a state of being that we'll achieve if we tick off enough boxes on our bucket list. In the classical Buddhist literature, two words are commonly used to explore the notion of happiness: *sukha* and *mudita*. In English, sukha certainly means happiness, but it also carries a connotation of ease, joy, and bliss in the very midst of processing the varied experiences of life. Mudita, on the other hand, implies a sense of inexplicable joy that arises from tending to the peace, well-being, and liberation of others. In both cases, happiness involves a sense of becoming rather than having become, of traversing rather than having arrived, and of instilling in others rather than cultivating for one's self.

So given all that, will Zen bring you happiness? The big point here is that happiness is intimately connected with liberation and awakening. But it's also *other* than that pinnacle state of awakening, which seems to arise in the process of being authentically in tune with the happenings of our life and in the service of others. Awakening is distinct from happiness, but in the experience of Zen practitioners, happiness tends to accompany awakening.

BEGINNER'S MIND

In 1970, the Japanese Zen sage Shunryu Suzuki immortalized an important notion in Zen practice via an anthology of his teachings entitled *Zen Mind, Beginner's Mind*. Suzuki believed that a beginner's mind offers many possibilities compared to an expert's mind, which offers few.

To engage the world with the mind of a beginner is to interact with the world as if it were ever new, instead of being constrained by the narratives of your previous experiences. Think of what it's like when you begin a new jigsaw puzzle. Your eyes can easily locate related pieces and place them accordingly. Later, once you're familiar with the image being assembled, you often find that a piece doesn't fit where you thought it would. A beginner's mind is much more likely to take an awakened perspective and transcend the malaise of familiarity—new eyes that haven't been working on the puzzle can frequently place the piece with ease. Conversely, it's the sense that we've seen it all, an endless loop of "same old, same old," that fuels the depression and melancholy that many people feel throughout life.

So much of our suffering, or dukkha, as discussed in chapter 1, arises from living in a simulated reality, one we construct because we think we know how things work. This is the "expert's mind" Suzuki spoke of. It can guide our awareness so that we refuse to see things as they truly are. This mindset keeps you from accepting things or experiences and responding to them accordingly. When we have the mind of the expert, it means that instead of seeing the world as it is, we see the world as *we* are. Instead of actually perceiving the world, we see it as we've always seen it. With an expert's mind, we come to feel like we're watching a mediocre film over and over again, on constant replay. And so we withdraw further and further into ourselves, rather than being drawn into relationships with the wide body of experiences that the world offers but that we don't allow ourselves to then perceive.

In many ways, the beginner's mind is the container of right view (from the Eightfold Path) and the bedrock of liberation. The beginner's mind wonders. The beginner's mind is capable of wandering, of exploring the horizons of change and unknowing. A central task of Zen practice is to become intimate and comfortable with unknowing and not trying to avoid it and its sometimes unsettling effects. The expert's mind tends to stagnate in the sludge of certainty. It's shielded from the discomfort of unknowing but unable to respond to the world as it really is; and so, it is prone to suffering.

The beginner's mind is not synonymous with naivete, however. We all accumulate experience during our lives that can aid in our comfort. But the beginner's mind relies on an experience-informed conception of reality only in the lightest and finest ways. With a beginner's mind, we always allow the actual world to inform our direct experience, and we meet it with the curious embrace of probing wonder. Indeed, we must never let our minds become so saturated with past experiences that we lose awareness of the living, and ultimately unpredictable, present moment.

ZEN AND MINDFULNESS

Some would half-jokingly postulate that Zen is perhaps more concerned with mind*less*ness than mindfulness; insomuch as a mind that is full leaves no room for genuine experience of the present, having filled itself with the conceptions of the past. Any type of meditation can risk this (that includes unchecked Zen practice)—namely, becoming a ritualized recollection of experiences and feelings rather than a live, perception-based engagement with reality in its current iteration. Zen as a path of mindfulness is particularly concerned with avoiding just that.

While there is a huge variety of methods offered under the banner of mindfulness in modern wellness paradigms and programs, very few of them are rooted in Zen. Rather, they are various iterations on a theme, ranging from orthodox Theravada Buddhism concepts to contemporary psychological tools constructed in academic research centers.

What perhaps most clearly delineates Zen methods from those of other schools and academic disciplines is the essentially goalless nature of the practice. *All* forms of meditation involve various parameters and instructions. Some mindfulness exercises follow a prescribed series of steps or techniques. Zen instructs that we should simply sit down, quiet down, and pay attention. Whatever happens in that space could rightfully be construed as Zen.

Practicing Zen is often described as a barebones method, one that may take longer to understand or even become familiar and comfortable with, compared to other meditative traditions. However, the demanding ambiguity of the Zen approach brings holistic engagement of the grand themes of faith, courage, and doubt. To nurture great faith means to employ relentless effort in the face of unknowing.

To nurture great courage means to summon a sense of boldness that leans into discomfort instead of avoiding it. To nurture great doubt means to always be wary of settling for momentary sufficiency, to instead challenge ourselves to keep progressing with the unfolding pace of reality itself. Together, these themes comprise the distinctive flavor of Zen practice.

PRACTICING ZEN

While the preceding pages have no doubt oriented you quite broadly to the Zen tradition, we will now begin to explore the actual practices that comprise it. The key Zen disciplines of the lineages that I have been trained in and authorized to represent (namely, spiritual direction with a competent guide, meditative inquiry, and koan introspection) will all be explored in some depth as this book progresses. Before that, though, we will survey the overall trajectory of a life of Zen practice through the guidance of two seminal masters of the Zen way, one ancient (Dongshan Liangjie) and one contemporary (Seung Sahn Haeng Won).

In attempting to create something of a prospectus for Zen practitioners to consult on their own sojourning, while also establishing a theoretical basis for Zen teachers to gauge the practice of students, the Tang dynasty Zen sage Dongshan Liangjie formulated a schema of five different stages, or significant milestones, that he called ranks. Dongshan's Five Ranks—(I) The Relative within the Absolute, (II) The Absolute within the Relative, (III) Coming from within the Absolute, (IV) Arrival at Mutual Integration, and (V) Unity Attained—have proven imminently helpful in aiding Zen students and teachers alike in evaluating their practice for centuries, while also proving somewhat cumbersome as a stand-alone instrument. Accordingly, in the twentieth century, Dongshan's teaching was reimagined by the preeminent Korean Zen Master Seung Sahn in the form of a familiar image: a compass.

Roughly estimating Dongshan's Five Ranks as five points on a compass or circle, Seung Sahn's teaching offers us a lens through which we can navigate our Zen journey as we advance toward, regress from, progress through, and eventually re-arrive variously at the points of 0°, 90°, 180°, 270°, and 360°. While both Dongshan and Seung Sahn offered their teaching primarily through poetry, Seung Sahn's system simplified Dongshan's assertions with simple images about the appearance and function of mountains and rivers common to the Zen tradition.

0°, the Relative within the Absolute (the First Rank)

Chiefly identifiable in newborns and animals, the first rank or point on the Zen compass can be conceived of through the traditional poetic image of "mountains as mountains and rivers as rivers." Here, human beings find themselves in utter accord with their instinctual urges and environmental factors. Here, when we're hungry, uncomfortable, afraid, tired, or otherwise in need, we cry, scream out, sleep, or procure beyond considerations of ethics. Here is where we explore the world through the gates of perception and before beginning to accumulate the assumptions that will deter us from our direct awareness of the world. At this point, we instinctively posit that *things simply are as they are*, as they appear to be. While most adults do not routinely dwell in this place, it is the primal iteration of mind from which great bravery and great tragedy can freely flow alike, and where we can find ourselves regressing to at the edges of our sanity.

90°, the Absolute within the Relative (the Second Rank)

Typically beginning in adulthood, this second rank's traditional poetic image tells us that "mountains are rivers, and rivers are mountains." This 90° point is one of conceptual thought, where we've explored the world enough to incur just enough experience to cognitively posit that *things might be other than they seem*. For many, Zen practice and spiritual journeying of all sorts begin at this point.

180°, Coming from within the Absolute (the Third Rank)

Once we've set foot on the Zen path and seemingly made some progress toward exploring its teachings and practices, with any luck we reach a significant realization:

Nothing is as it seems. The traditional poetic image at this third rank tells us that both "mountains and rivers disappear." We come to know that our conceptions are just that: weak representations of reality that typically fail to even remotely mirror what they claim to be true. Our conceptual castings of reality fall apart, and perhaps for the first time we can emerge as adults primed with a beginner's mind. This third rank is the first real marker of correct practice.

270°, Arrival at Mutual Integration (the Fourth Rank)

Progressing through the third rank is indeed a difficult task. One can find themselves hopeless and helpless with the donning of the realizations intrinsic to "Coming from within the Absolute," and the wise guidance of a teacher or community can be exceptionally helpful at this point. And when it happens that we are able to move through the third rank of 180°, we find ourselves diametrically opposed to where were when we set foot on the Zen path. Here, the traditional poetic image tells us that somehow "mountains grow out of the sky, and rivers flow upward." Instead of merely theorizing that things *might* be other than they seem, you know—have veritably experienced— that in fact *things are other than they seem.* The world, the universe, and reality at large are far more malleable, indistinct, and interconnected than our conceptions would (and did) have us believe. We find ourselves taken up by the wonder and freedom that perhaps we once knew and now know again with agency. And still, caution is to be entertained. The only thing more difficult on the path than progressing through the third rank is progressing through the fourth and not becoming distracted by liberation and unknowing that might mask what is yet to be understood and attained.

360°, Unity Attained (the Fifth Rank)

Should we stay the course, we may find our self once again at 0°, known now as 360°: Unity Attained. Here, certainly things are not as they seem, and somehow they are also not otherwise! Here, *things simply are as they are,* and as the traditional poetic image would note, "mountains are mountains, and rivers are rivers." At this fifth rank, things are as they are, and we are as we are, with and aligned to reality—where, having long traversed the path outlined in the five ranks, we can perhaps actualize a sense of contentment and "enough."

To practice Zen is to practice life, to return time and time again to the processes, places, people, and events that we know intimately but disregard. Zen is a process of reexamining and not assuming so that you feel the ground beneath your feet in every given moment instead of ignoring it. Why? Because the present moment is the only place that our lives really exist and unfold.

A BEGINNER'S STORY: ZEN PRACTICE

A few years after I had finally decided to commit myself fully to the practice of Zen as a very young person, I was given the responsibility of hosting a retreat at my then-fledgling Zen center. I was also responsible for organizing the travel of my teacher and the retreat leader.

On the way to pick up my teacher, traffic to the airport was minimal, and the flight had arrived on time. However, on the way back to the center, traffic ground to a halt. For several minutes I apologized, opining on various schemes to reroute around the traffic difficulties so we could arrive on time at the center, where many people were already waiting for the retreat to begin.

The teacher listened to my fretting and scheming for a good half hour, relatively unmoved. But when I let out a sigh as we rounded yet another corner to a dead stop, he suddenly roared from his gut something to the tune of, "Where are you?!"

I paused my ranting and, really, my thinking. Seconds that passed like hours of ignorance-cleaving silence passed, and I sat bewildered.

"You are right here, right now," he stated. "Not on some other road, not at the Zen center, and nothing can change that. Don't make where you're going more important than where you are. Ever."

I quickly learned that the formalities of the retreat could wait, for in their delay, authentic practice had already begun for all of us in the car and at the center.

HOW TO MEDITATE

As alluded to elsewhere in this text, Zen meditation instruction often can seem minimal and even insufficient. In Zen centers and temples around the globe, emphasis tends to be placed more on the *how* in this regard, rather than on the precise *what* to do. Often, when we are taught how to sit down we are told that we should quiet down and pay attention, if even only to the teacher's cues at first.

Nevertheless, here are some guidelines that can be helpful for beginners. Collectively, these form the container of Zen practice known as zazen in Japanese, or "sitting Zen" in English.

Be consistent. When establishing a meditation practice, constancy is key. Typically, Zen meditation sessions range from twenty to thirty minutes in length. However, it's better to practice for ten minutes at the same time each day than to try to sit for thirty minutes sporadically. When you can consistently practice for ten minutes every day, gradually work your way up to twenty or thirty minutes, and perhaps from one to two periods of meditation a day.

Attend to your posture. The specific posture taken up in Zen meditation need not be a classical full lotus position, or cross-legged posture on a cushion on the floor. Rather, what is most important is to tend to a few principles that promote comfort and alertness in the practice of meditation. Generally speaking, your back should be straight (as if your head were suspended from a string) and supported by the structure of your body, rather than by any furniture (such as the back of a chair) if possible. Your knees should be positioned slightly lower than your waist, to open up the belly and hip flexor muscles, promoting your ability to breathe fully, and to adequately circulate blood and oxygen. If you're sitting in a chair, your feet should be flat on the floor.

Remember your hand placement and gaze. In the practice of Zen meditation, your hands should be relaxed and open, resting on your lap with your left hand facing upward, nested atop the right open palm. Draw your thumbs together to slightly and gently touch, forming a circle. This is known as a dhyana mudra, or the meditation hand symbol. Your eyes should be gently open, attuned to reality rather than to the barrage of thoughts easily accessible behind your eyelids. Let your gaze fall naturally in front of you, at about a 45° downward angle, focused on nothing in particular but not drifting about.

Let yourself breathe. Breathing should be deep but at a natural and comfortable rhythm. Inhale and exhale through your nose if possible, so that your tongue rests gently behind your front teeth, touching the upper palate. Employ your diaphragm by breathing into your lower belly, allowing your abdomen to gently but visibly expand upon inhalation and fall on exhalation. It's important to breathe at a comfortable, natural rate and rhythm, typically between twelve and twenty respirations per minute. You should not be on the cusp of gasping for air between breaths nor hyperventilating.

Adjust as needed. If you must move during meditation, move slowly and intentionally, whether scratching an itch or stretching a knee. It can be a useful practice to explore an impulse to move or scratch before simply reacting to it. While discomfort is an expected and frequent companion of a still, seated meditation practice, that doesn't mean meditation should take a masochistic tone. Tend to the needs of your body with compassion and intentionality. But also be aware that our minds are particularly adept at forging excuses to not engage this type of essentially goalless practice.

Correct when necessary. In the beginning stages of practice, especially if you are practicing on your own, it may be necessary to return to these directions several times to ensure that something isn't being missed. In a traditional group Zen training environment, typically a senior student is assigned to offer gentle corrections on posture and wakefulness, which are both easy to lose in beginning stages of practice. When practicing on your own, you must be your own vigilant attendant. Invite yourself back into proper form when a lapse occurs. Know that the mind follows breath and posture, just as breath and posture follow the mind. When your posture is engaged and upright, so, too, will be your mind, and if your mind is calm and attentive, so, too, will be your breathing.

Go easy on yourself. As mentioned, the life and practice of the Zen teacher—and therefore of the Zen student—is but one continuous mistake. Give yourself and this book (your teacher for a time) some compassion and grace for the inevitable volley of missteps to come. They, too, happen only in the immaculate space that is this very moment.

A BEGINNER'S STORY: ZEN MEDITATION

A student once approached a famous Zen Master and explained, "Teacher, I really don't like the dhyana mudra. I can't stop thinking about it, and my practice is disturbed. Can you please assign me a different mudra to use in my meditation practice?" The dhyana mudra is the circular hand position used in Zen meditation.

The teacher replied, "Of course, no problem!" Drawing his right arm and hand up and over his head to touch his left shoulder, the Zen Master then drew his left arm and hand behind his back to touch his right with the backside of his palm and said, "This will be your new mudra!"

Looking aghast, the student replied, "Thank you for your instruction, teacher. I now think that the dhyana mudra is okay after all." The teacher responded, "Oh, okay. Very good."

In the practice of Zen, many of our forms and postures are very exacting, frequently offering but one manner of performance. This can seem to strike at the very heart of what we deem to be our most prized possession—namely, our sense of personal agency. What we are quick to forget, however, is that this very sense of personal freedom and choice delivers us to the practice of Zen as we seek to overcome our suffering and dissatisfaction in life.

Albert Einstein is said to have once observed, "We cannot solve our problems with the same thinking we used when we created them." That's true enough to drive home this point: Zen practice works when it is practiced as it is offered. Your personal resistance to any number of Zen forms is inevitable; it happens to all of us.

That resistance, though, is a precious place of realization, if we allow ourselves to examine it before we respond (let alone react) to it. The adequate response may be to simply uphold, for a time, the tension between practicing and being dissatisfied with it.

ZEN KOANS: THE SOUND OF ONE HAND CLAPPING

There are few things more intriguing in the Zen tradition than the koan. Strictly speaking, the word *koan* is a Japanese term that means "public case." In essence, koans are case studies of the nature and functioning of the awakened mind. Think of a koan as an invitation into new ways of being. They teach us to accord with reality as it has been known to the sages of this tradition throughout time.

Contrary to popular belief, there is no set answer or response to a koan that is universally accepted. The point is not to respond to the satisfaction of a teacher but to enter into the koan and become one with the vision of reality that it portrays. Teachers are often cast as essential to the practice of koans, a perspective I am mostly keen to agree with. But in a very real way, the true evidence of someone realizing the awakened vision of a koan rests in the personal experience of the student who is wrestling with it.

Koans ask us to reexamine our most fundamental assumptions of reality, to set aside the conventional, and, rather than discard our thinking, reinvest it into this very moment. In doing so, we recalibrate our perception and uproot the conditioning that has thus far informed our neuroses and fueled our malcontent. Koans can set into motion the maturation of an ever-deepening communion with an awakened reality.

One of the most famous Zen koans posits that when two hands clap, there is a sound, and further inquires, What is the sound of one hand clapping? Indeed, what *is* the sound of one hand clapping?

HOW TO WORK WITH KOANS

Throughout this book, a handful of koans will be presented alongside a variety of other exercises to help augment your foray into the world of Zen practice. While the medium of a book is perhaps not the most ideal mechanism for facilitating koan practice, there is much precedent for engaging a koan essentially on your own.

There is no one right way to work with a koan. However, one method that I find to be particularly efficacious is to survey the classical collections of koans that are widely available online, or the handful presented in this text. Find one that particularly speaks to you in some way, and commit it to memory.

This is always the first step in koan practice: making the koan a part of your physiology via memorization, so it can be carried with you wherever you go and accessed at any time and in any context.

The very act of mental and/or verbal repetition that memorization requires is itself an initial method of practice. As you memorize, you're simply revisiting the case over and over, tending to whatever images or thoughts it may provoke, and again returning to the case itself.

This can be done in zazen (sitting meditation), while cooking, while driving, or simply in passing, whenever your memory of the koan may be propelled into your active consciousness throughout the day. Pay particular attention to those moments and their implications on your thinking.

Remember that while eureka moments can be genuinely profound, Zen practice is fundamentally a practice of returning. The process of returning to our koan with a sense of great doubt, especially after we convince ourselves (time and again) that we have thoroughly understood and digested it, is the basis of a particularly fertile and precious practice. Eventually, in time and if possible, a duly qualified teacher is highly recommended to deepen your koan work.

KEY TAKEAWAYS

- Zen teaches us that happiness is a process and an experiential orientation, rather than an immutable reality.

- Happiness is connected with awakening but distinct from it.

- A beginner's mind perceives the world as it is and finds wonder in it; the expert's mind sees what it expects and avoids unknowing.

- The key disciplines of practicing Zen are spiritual direction with a competent guide, meditative inquiry, and koan introspection.

- A koan does not have a universally set answer or response. Memorizing a koan is a helpful first step, as the process of practicing with koans involves revisiting them again and again.

CHAPTER 3

ZEN HAPPINESS IN THE MORNING

In this chapter, we shift from examining the historical context and philosophical structure of the Zen tradition and move into the realm of its application and ongoing implementation in your life. Each of the following chapters will examine stories, exercises, and case studies in the form of koans that relate to four phases of a hypothetical modern day. We'll begin by inviting Zen practice into a typically auto-piloted morning routine. As you study these pages, keep in mind that although the exercises are related to each chapter's area of focus, the principles presented are universally applicable to Zen practice.

Tam: An All Too Typical Morning

It was a Monday morning, not unlike any of the thousands that Tam had experienced in her life. Sure, the recent shift in daylight savings time had rendered the sunlight a little dimmer when her six a.m. alarm went off. Sure, she'd arrived home later than anticipated last night, thanks to a delayed flight on the final leg returning from a weekend trip. But this was a Monday after all, and well-rested alertness was far from what Tam had come to expect on such days.

Snoozing her alarm for a third time, Tam tried to roll her tired body from underneath her blankets, groggily asking herself, "How can it be time to get up already?" Her body ached and her joints were stiff, and Tam's eyelids felt like lead as she tried to open them to catch the faint glimmer of morning light through the window blinds. As she stumbled to the bathroom, Tam's mind was already racing through her list of to-dos for the day. Her heart took up its now-familiar stressed-out and accelerated rhythm, and then Tam's alarm started loudly squawking, the last snooze timer having run out. Sprinting back to her bedside to silence the alarm, Tam only then consciously realized that she'd hit the snooze button more than once and was already running late.

After rushing through a familiar shower and dressing routine, Tam ran downstairs. She grabbed an overripe banana from the counter on her way out the door, thinking, *This will have to do for breakfast today.* Barely remembering to lock her door behind her, Tam set out to meet the day tired, frazzled, and hungry.

PUTTING SNOOZE TO REST

In Zen centers and temples, there is no snooze button. The sound of the bell, drum, or clacker wakes and moves the community. If you don't keep up, the day moves on without you, and your place at the temple may become compromised. To meet this reality, Zen trainees learn to respond to the various sounds of the temple, beyond the illusion of choice.

In your daily life, when your morning alarm sounds, the Zen response is simply to sit up and plant your feet firmly on the floor. After your feet meet the ground, your next response is to take a breath and stand up. After that, you take several steps around your room, proceeding to bathe, dress, and conduct any other personal activities to prepare for the day.

Breaking the task of rising into a manageable and practicable chain of responses reprograms the brain to live in accord with reality and your commitments to it. You set that morning alarm for a reason. And the common mental protestation of "five more minutes" ultimately does not serve that reason, nor is it conducive to meeting your day.

MINDFUL MOVEMENT

Zen practice that neglects the body ultimately neglects the mind; there is no real dichotomy between the two. When you wake up and physically get moving, the activity is good for your setting your mind in motion as well.

To invite this principle into your morning routine, after you stand up, begin to mindfully move your body.

Start from the top of your head and work systematically to the tips of your toes as you are able, following this sequence:

1. Begin by successively moving your eyebrows up and down, flaring your nostrils, lifting the corners of your mouth, and opening and closing your jaw. Gently bend your neck forward, back, and to each side. Shrug your shoulders up and down. Draw your shoulder blades together while straightening your spine.

2. Next, gently twist to the left and right from your waist, allowing your arms to sway from the shoulders with each twist.

3. Bend forward at the waist, reaching toward your toes (don't force yourself to touch them; bend as far as is comfortable). Draw back and place your hands on your hips; gently stretch backward, bending back at the waist as far as is safe and comfortable. Repeat this several times.

4. Keep your hands on the hips for a moment, and make gentle circles by moving through the full motion range of your hip joints, circling left and then right.

5. Place your hands on your knees. Gently bend forward while bending your knees and moving them in small circles, to the left and then right. Squat down and stand again several times.

6. Stand on one foot (or sit, if balancing is difficult) and gently articulate the opposite ankle, foot, and toes. Switch feet and repeat.

MINDFUL THIRDS

Proper nutrition is an absolute necessity for those seeking to train their bodies and minds in the way of Zen. The goal of this practice isn't to break down dietary recommendations of any Zen tradition. Rather, it's to call your mind toward the necessity of taking in proper nutrients each day in a mindful way. Here are the guidelines to follow:

Think in thirds. Eat your meals in a formal, relatively slow-paced, and complete way. Little should be wasted, including time. The rule of thumb for eating in the Zen tradition is to fill the belly one-third with food and one-third with water, leaving room for one-third air. This formula makes for easy digestion.

Use your senses. Eating mindfully is the process of eating with your eyes first, then with your nose and hands (and utensils), followed by your mouth, throat, and stomach. In the Zen tradition, eat one bite at a time and take in the food's physical qualities (color, smell, temperature, texture, taste).

Pace yourself. Chew the food thoroughly, swallowing it completely before moving to take another bite. Slowing down your eating processes keeps the body's digestive processes from becoming overwhelmed. In doing so, mindful eating allows you to feel nourished in tandem with the amount of food you eat, rather than waiting for the sensations of your mind and body to catch up with your food intake (which frequently leads to digestive discomfort). Remind yourself that eating healthfully is not just about what you eat or even how much you eat but also *how* you eat.

YOUR MORNING KOAN: YUNMEN'S GOOD DAY

"Before or after the full moon, every day is a good day!"

This koan comes from the *Blue Cliff Record* anthology of Zen koans. It's spoken by famed Zen Master Yunmen addressing an assembly of Zen students.

While the historical and cultural context is somewhat difficult to penetrate, Zen Master Yunmen has become perhaps most famous for his capping phrase: "Every day is a good day." For many students of Zen, this phrase elicits either fervent contest or zealous embrace. Both reactions are perfectly natural but are also prone to missing the point. How is every day a good day? What does that mean? Was September 11, 2001, a good day? (Review How to Work with Koans, page 38, if you have trouble getting started.)

ZAZEN (SEATED MEDITATION)

The three preceding exercises were primarily concerned with setting an appropriate container for the rest of your day to unfold within. The true Zen adept makes time for formal practice on a daily basis, to create space for the fullness of a Zen life to be lived out. For this exercise, you make that space.

Contemplate (in alignment with your typical scheduled demands) the best waking time for routinely practicing seated meditation for ten, twenty, or even thirty minutes each day. Generally speaking, seated meditation should not be practiced in the immediate wake of a meal (so as to avoid potential drowsiness) and should be practiced at a relatively consistent time so as to establish a habit.

The ideal meditation period lasts around thirty minutes, but it is more than okay to begin with five- or ten-minute periods. Just be sure to do so habitually. For specific instructions, review "How to Meditate" in chapter 2 (page 32).

THE MONDO AS A TOUCHSTONE

In addition to seated meditation, the Zen tradition offers a nearly infinite array of practices that take place around the core discipline of seated meditation. One is the recitation of various poems and utterances (called gathas) at various parts of the day, as guideposts and touchstones for cultivating an awakened mindset. Zen Master

Yunmen's short supposition "Every day is a good day" is a possible mindful touchstone.

Keeping Yunmen's words in your heart and mind on a daily basis forces you to confront the conundrum of your experiences. It also allows you to recall the promise of the Zen tradition while paving the way for the hundreds of hours you'll spend meditating over the course of your life, invoking them with a single touch phrase.

Here are two ways (among many) to enact this practice:

- Following your daily practice of seated meditation, practice reciting "Every day is a good day." Repeat it out loud or in your mind throughout the course of your day.

- Recite the phrase in place of a seated meditation. In this way, the phrase can be practiced as a koan or, more specifically, a mondo, the focal point of a koan. It serves as a ritual acknowledgment that we've sat with our minds in formal practice for a time.

GAINING COMFORT WITH UNKNOWING

At this point in your Zen journey, it's appropriate to introduce the formal practice of tending to unknowing. To gain comfort with unknowing is perhaps simultaneously the most rudimentary and most advanced Zen practice. And the most intimate.

As you progress, there will be days when you will not want to practice, and you will lose track of your own motivation. Here are some methods for moving through these moments:

Use your senses. Without knowing how or why, persist, and return to the processes of meticulous tending to the phenomena that befalls your experience. What are you perceiving? Hold these things gently, peer into them without expectation, and persist.

Say it out loud. The great Zen Master Seung Sahn famously taught his students to invoke the phrase "Don't know" to help propel them through these moments of losing momentum. Repeat those words, remembering that mere intellectual not knowing and all-encompassing, experiential unknowing are very different. We should uphold the latter, not fear it, even if it accompanies the former.

Press pause. When you feel overwhelmed with unknowing, it can be a useful to pause your progression into newer and newer methods and keep with your current practice. When you become comfortable with it, then it may be time to progress not just deeper into your current practices but more broadly into the expanding array of practices that constitute the Zen tradition.

DHARMA FOR THE MORNING: CARRYING A YOUNG WOMAN

A well-known Zen story finds two monks walking along a path one day, when they come across a navigable ravine that has been flooded by recent rains. Waiting at the ravine is a beautiful young woman dressed in fine silk, unable to cross and continue on her way. The elder monk offers to carry her across so she will not ruin her clothing. The woman accepts, and after crossing, she and the monks immediately part ways.

After a time, the younger monk, who has been agitated and restless since leaving the woman at the ravine, speaks in a loud voice, saying, "Older brother! I cannot believe you carried that young woman across the ravine. Our precepts are very clear in teaching us to not have any contact with the opposite sex. How could you do such a thing?"

The elder monk turns to the younger monk and instructs, "I put the woman down on the other side of the ravine. Why are you still carrying her?"

MANTRA RECITATION

At times you may find it difficult to settle into the discipline of seated meditation. Perhaps the notion of sitting still, let alone doing so without any measure of productivity or accomplishment, seems all but impossible. In times like these, mantra practice can be very useful. The word *mantra* in Sanskrit means "a tool" (tra) for "the mind" (manas). Mantras can range from short words or even syllables to long phrases, repeated again and again in cyclical patterns to achieve a specific outcome. The goal is to cut through what is known as discursive thinking in the Zen tradition.

At this stage in your practice, the content of the mantra—the words and syllables that comprise it—are of little importance. What matters is that those words or syllables don't connect directly with any stream of conceptual thought. It has been said that even "Coca-Cola, Coca-Cola, Coca-Cola" could be a sufficient mantra, as long as you can avoid the mental imagery of sugary beverages.

Popular beginning mantras in the Zen tradition include:

- "Om Mani Padme Hum" ("The jewel is in the lotus" in Sanskrit).

- "Kwan Se Um Bo Sal" ("One who perceives the sounds of the world" in Sino-Korean).

- "Gate Gate Paragate Parasamgate Bodhi Svaha" (Sanskrit for "Going, going, going on beyond, going completely beyond awakening. So be it!").

Shorter mantras might include "Om nam," which is not directly translatable. Even so, it's celebrated for the quality of its sounds as "The mantra of the universe in its purity."

For this practice, it doesn't matter so much what mantra you choose, just that you choose one.

- Practice gently invoking the mantra with your voice for up to several minutes before settling into a seated meditation session.

- Repeat the mantra slowly and audibly, perhaps at a pace of three recitations per exhalation.

- If you find your mind drifting, simply and gently return to the mantra, feeling it in your chest, in your throat, on your tongue, and in your ears.

- Repeat your mantra for a minute or two. Traditionally, mantras are often recited in units of 108 recitations.

- Once you've finished, you may come to a natural place of drifting from reciting the mantra into sitting in relative silence—the proper progression from mantra to meditation.

COMMUTING WITH ATTENTION AND INTENTION

We often find that the capacity to not be present comes to us quite naturally. How many times have you driven to work and not remembered a single detail about what happened between point A and point B? The purpose of this practice is to cultivate presence in the midst of those familiar events that we tend to tune out. On your commute, be it daily or intermittently, try being present without any distractions. No radio, podcasts, or audiobooks, no text messages or emails. Just driving or sitting, taking in the fullness of the experience. The process is simple:

1. Abandon productivity and boredom for a time, and just be with the experience of driving, taking the train, or sitting in a carpool.

2. When you arrive at your destination, pause to recount the experience in your head. Note at least three specific details you experienced that you might have otherwise missed. It could be as simple as the color of the trees or the thinning paint on a patch of highway, or as profound as the smile (or frown) on the face of a stranger. In any case, be, notice, and remember.

WHAT IS THIS?

The Zen instruction to be present with the fullness of our lives as they unfold, and to not carry around experiences and thoughts rooted in the near or distant past, is clear. But as you are no doubt realizing, that's a difficult instruction to follow.

In the Korean tradition, holding a profound question (such as "What is this?") is known as hwadu practice. Holding the question in your mind with such resolution and immediacy that there is nothing to do but tend to the question, without solving it, is a way of learning to abide in unknowing.

Focus on the question. When you find your mind adrift, or you're struggling to be present for this moment, employ the question "What is this?" Hold it deeply.

Use your senses. In the beginning stages of practicing with the hwadu question, answer using simple observations rooted in you six senses. Name what you see, hear, smell, taste, feel, and think. Used in this way, the hwadu is a grounding process, keeping you in the present.

Follow where it leads. As you reach a more advanced practice, you may find that the very asking of the question invites you into an indescribable fullness of experience, one that can be met only with the response of wonderous unknowing, of experiential "don't know." That is, until perhaps someday an indescribable knowing appears: the stuff that Zen Masters might call awakening.

KEY TAKEAWAYS

- The morning hours are a particularly important time to pay attention to our Zen practice, because they form the container of experience for the day.

- Subtle forms of morning practice include waking up with our feet on the ground, moving our bodies, eating mindfully, welcoming unknowing, and commuting without distraction.

- More formal and overt practices include seated meditation, koan introspection, mantra practice, and probing into our experience with the hwadu question "What is this?"

CHAPTER 4

ZEN HAPPINESS OUT AND ABOUT

Our modern lives are thoroughly inundated with nearly infinite ways to stay busy. We're constantly dividing our attention to get more done, and yet somehow stretched for time. Seldom are we engaged in just one task; even our commuting and leisure time competes with cell phone alerts and messaging. In this chapter, we will explore how Zen's disciplines can bring intentionality and awareness amid the hustle of daily life, especially in its unplanned and otherwise cluttered moments. Happiness, after all, is not something to manifest on command when it's convenient or expected. Zen teaches us that happiness is an experience that dawns in our lives when we're mindfully engaged with the present moment.

Addison: An All Too Typical Trip Out and About

Life for Addison was always on the go. The Zen notion of focusing on any one thing at a time proved difficult for her. Addison frequently complained to her wife of having no time, between needing to think two steps ahead in managing their child's school and extracurricular schedules, tending to the family dog, and meeting the demands of her own full-time job . . . not to mention a full slate of ongoing household tasks and a committed relationship deserving of attention. Addison had little time left for herself, and when she was not running from one task to the next, she did not know what to do with her so-called downtime. Some unnamed, amorphous responsibility to come always seemed to loom on Addison's mind, even when she *knew* it was okay to take a pause for a moment and just be.

All of the shuffle in Addison's life was beginning to take a toll on her health. After a checkup in response to some intermittent chest pain, Addison's doctor advised that stress was a likely culprit. The prescription seemed easier said than done: a course in mindfulness and a good dose of slowing down, not yet available in pharmaceutical form. Addison knew that her current pace of life was unsustainable but struggled to decide where or how to begin making meaningful changes. Merely thinking about it seemed to cause even more stress. Before any more thought could be given to the idea, Addison's phone was already ringing, with her son on the line reminding her that it was time to pick him up from chess club. Addison was quickly whisked back into the unpredictable rhythm of a life in progress.

MAKING A HABIT

From the earliest stages of the Buddhist tradition, a *habit* (in this context, referring not to a thing we do but to the word's older meaning: a religious garment) has been a central touch point for practice. The discipline of wearing some form of habit relating to Zen can prove both easily doable and useful to new practitioners. One such example is the use of a mala, or token string of beads.

Mala beads are widely available online and in various stores today; you may have seen them worn by a friend who has an interest in Buddhism or as a fashion statement. They come in many varieties, the most traditional being a strand of 108 beads. For this practice, obtain a set of mala beads or, if that's not practical for you, some another unique piece of apparel that you can wear routinely but isn't already part of your wardrobe.

Wear your habit to call your mind to your mindful practice throughout the day. Each time you find your attention drawn to the beads/necklace/scarf/whatever, through its weight, through adjusting its position, or even when someone asks about it, take a moment to enjoy several slow, deep breaths—or at least the spirit of them, as circumstances might demand!

PUTTING TECHNOLOGY TO PRACTICE

It would be easy to cast the technology common to our everyday lives as subversive to the aims and objectives of Zen practice. But Zen is not intrinsically a discipline for Luddites. In Addison's story, she struggles to tend to all of the rings, beeps, and jingles that demand her attention. Such alerts could be cast as invasions upon our consciousness. Approached through the lens of practice, however, technological demands can be recast as invitations to mindful awareness.

For this practice, choose a daily alert that is common in your life (perhaps a text message alert or your phone's ringtone) and begin responding to it with a pause of at least three full seconds, taking time to breathe in and out fully before addressing the alert. As this becomes routine, try it with other alerts or cues.

For the next step, interject a momentary body scan into your alert-answering practice. For this, in addition to a pause for a breath, take time to examine the points of tension in your body and voluntarily relax them before tending to the demand that the alert is tied to.

When this response is second nature, set alarms at various intervals with no other purpose than to invite you to add a moment of practicing awareness to your daily routine.

BEING THERE WHILE GETTING THERE

For both new and established practitioners alike, it's tempting to fall into the dualistic trap of dividing your life into "practice" and "everything else." We might look at life as an array of experiences, commitments, and responsibilities that somehow draw us away from bliss, but with momentary blips of joy as counterbalance. The Zen school, however, posits that life—*all* of life—belongs to a common and contiguous fabric—namely, that of reality itself. Your Zen practice is merely the way of engaging with life that illumines it as such and thereby opens a door to meaning and integration.

Zen Master Seung Sahn is known to have taught that "a good situation is a bad situation and a bad situation is a good situation," relatively speaking. For this practice, keep Seung Sahn's words in mind and recall an unsavory experience, either one from recent memory or one that's had a lasting impact. Examining this experience, consider what causes and conditions set it into motion. What different sides might there be to the situation? If this experience were occurring today, how might it be accessible to, or considered as, your Zen practice?

The past is ultimately unchangeable. Our regard for it, though, is entirely malleable. While examining the selected situation, try lifting the corner of your lips into a smile. Offer a chuckle where a sigh or a complaint might otherwise be attempting to form. Connecting to this moment, breathe fully into your experience and monitor how your affectation is easily changed or easily triggered into resistance.

YOUR OUT AND ABOUT KOAN: EMPEROR WU'S MERIT

Fifteen hundred years ago, the Chinese emperor Wu of Liang converted to Buddhism and quickly set about patronizing the religion. Having built countless temples, funded the translation of numerous scriptures, and sponsored scores of missionaries, the emperor was keen to meet the itinerant founding master of the Zen Buddhist school, Bodhidharma, who had recently made his way to China. Upon their meeting, the emperor inquired of the monk, "I have made Buddhism the national religion, have built numerous temples and monasteries, translated many scriptures, and converted millions to Buddhism. What merit have I thereby attained?" Bodhidharma replied, "No merit whatsoever." The emperor inquired, "Perhaps then I don't fully understand the teaching of the Buddha. How do you understand it?" Bodhidharma replied without hesitation, "In vast emptiness, no holiness."

Remember, the starting point of the koan is often bewilderment. This is how koans work and are worked within authentic Zen teaching and lineage.

SETTING EXPECTATIONS

In the beginning stages of Zen practice, many people are taken up with great hope for what the results of their efforts may be. We may envision ourselves as quickly ascending to some transcendent state wherein our lives are utterly transformed, but such lofty expectations are all but destined to be met with hearty disappointment. In spiritual pursuits, as in life generally, there are few fast passes, and the transformation of a life is a lifelong vocation. Should we wish to avoid Emperor Wu's bewilderment, then, we must be intentional about setting our expectations in accord with reality.

For this practice, take time to ask yourself sincerely:

What am I hoping to achieve through the practice of Zen?

When do I hope to realize such achievement?

What (or even who) am I trying to outrun?

In what ways do I believe such running, even if successful, will impact my life?

For some, the posing of these questions may take place while holding this book in a momentary contemplative pause. Others may find it useful to sit in a quiet place and take up each question one by one, at a time when they won't be disturbed. It may be helpful to journal with these questions, rather than simply ponder them mentally, or even record your spoken answers and revisit them later. As with all practices, follow your heart and pay special attention to those miraculous moments of discomfort that may arise. There is almost always significance to the areas of our practice that we find off-putting or even superfluous.

Common spiritual idiomatic wisdom suggests that "wherever you go, there you are." In becoming aware of the dreamlike and magical aspirations that we may hold for our Zen practice, we can realign those hopes to reality, and thereby avoid substantial disappointment. And, perhaps, actually make substantial progress in our Zen cultivation.

ESTABLISHING A DEDICATED PRACTICE SPACE

A dedicated physical space to support your practice can prove very helpful. And while certainly the practice of Zen is entirely accessible regardless of outward conditions, proper outward conditions can add wheels to a journey otherwise only able to be traveled by foot.

For this practice, establish a dedicated practice place for yourself, be it a room, a corner, or even a portion of a desk. Dedicated practice places can, over time, provide a route to nearly immediate centered and refined states of mind, compared to trying to access such states amid the spaces used for life's other busy processes. While this may seem counterintuitive in a chapter dedicated to implementing the Zen practice "out and about," having a place or even several places (at home, at work, or else-where) dedicated to your practice can greatly support the reclamation of a centered state when life otherwise might sway you far from course.

In addition to the practical concerns of the physical space itself—a quiet, comfortable, private place is helpful—consider ornamenting your practice space with some symbols or tools of Zen practice, such as an image of a Buddha, a string of mala beads, a candle or incense burner, a book of sacred writ, or even a small mirror to remind yourself that every step of the way is in fact the way itself, especially this very moment reflected back to you.

PRACTICING FOR OTHERS

The next time someone cuts you off in traffic, rolls their eyes in your general direction, or perhaps sends a rude email or impatiently honks their horn at you, it's your cue to enact this practice.

1. Remind yourself that in our shared world, which is often strewn with chaos and lacking in kindness, you may be the only beacon of present-moment-rooted awareness, compassion, and patience that the other person encounters on this day (or even in this week).

2. Instead of responding to their anger or rudeness in kind, find a way to respond with intentional warmth or compassion. This might mean a friendly smile and wave, an apology for your (perceived) mistake, or just letting them get on with their day without confronting them about their possibly misplaced aggression.

MULTITASKING

While the general notion of multitasking may at first seem to be anathema to the Zen tradition, which is so often equated to single-pointed attention and absorption, engaging in a variety of tasks simultaneously is an undeniable demand of life, modern and otherwise. As a natural demand of life, multitasking is, then, agreeable to Zen practice—though it's worth noting that, strictly speaking, humans don't so much multitask as move rapidly back and forth from one activity to another.

For this practice, choose a day to identify the minute gaps of time between the seemingly simultaneous activities and demands that you engage in while going about your usual routine.

For example:

Note how you move between listening, talking, and walking while having a conversation on your cell phone.

Pay mind to the shifts in attention that take place during a routine drive, as your awareness jumps from the road ahead to the dashboard to the rearview mirror.

Notice the movement of your attention when you attempt to eat a meal on the go or while working on something else. When do you taste the food on your tongue, and when are you browsing your email inbox or watching for the traffic light to change?

Contemplate the liminal space that connects these activities and the means by which that moment of task-switching becomes overlooked, thereby merging the separate tasks into a single event. Awareness enables the possibility of intention, and intentional awareness is the path of practice. In Zen, nothing should be overlooked, and the ways that our minds operate should be continually explored, to bring us toward an integrated expression of practice that continues to deepen.

CUTTING YOURSELF (AND EVERYONE ELSE) SOME SLACK

In the story on page 68, Zen Master Seung Sahn found himself confronted at breakfast by a student for seemingly existing at odds with his own teaching. While in short order the Zen Master was able to guide his student into a fuller view of awakened living, it is easy to relate to the student who simply sought to resolutely apply the teachings he had been offered. Life is comprised more of exceptions than rules, though, and more shades of gray than black-and-white binaries. Cultivating grace toward yourself and others instead of finding fault is a requirement for traversing the Zen path long term. This practice will help you foster that necessary kindness.

1. In your mind's eye, call up an image of someone (if not yourself) whom you feel totally positive toward.

2. Visualize them for several moments, and give way to the array of emotions and sensations that they elicit for you.

3. Breathing in and out deeply, with each respiration wish for this person to be happy, healthy, and well.

4. Continuing to breathe deeply, turn your attention to a person who raises slightly less positive feelings, and repeat the exercise.

5. Repeat the steps, moving in order to a completely neutral person, a slightly negative person, and finally to a person whom you feel almost or completely negative toward.

6. Repeat a final time, directing your attention to all beings in the universe.

Traditionally, this practice is called *metta* or *loving-kindness* practice, and over time you'll be able to shorten the process and employ it with difficult persons in a moment, while generally softening your disposition toward fellow sojourners on the human path.

SPIRITUAL FRIENDSHIP

The Buddha and his attendant, Ananda, were once walking down a path when Ananda posited to the Buddha that he had discerned that spiritual friendship comprised at least half of the spiritual path. The Buddha paused and then corrected Ananda, saying, "Ananda, say not so. Spiritual friendship is the whole of the path."

Spirituality and Zen practice in general are intensely personal endeavors, and indeed endeavors that no one can take up for you. But it's also true that Zen practice is ultimately best taken up with spiritual friendship: the support and counsel of peers and elders who can relate to your challenges and successes. Hence the existence of teachers and centers of practice, both often requiring us to get out and about, if not from our actual locales than from the limitations of our own interior, solitary lives.

For this practice, ask yourself:

What might I gain from a spiritual friendship or connection with another person?

In what aspects of my practice do I find myself in need of support, guidance, or even challenge?

Would it be more helpful to connect with a teacher, a mentor, or a peer?

Would I prefer connecting over secular commonalities or a shared spiritual ethos?

Noting the answers to these questions and any resistance to them, begin searching for opportunities online or in person to engage fellow wayfarers in a consistent manner and thus gain the blessings and challenges of intentional community.

KEY TAKEAWAYS

- The busyness of modern life can come to fully integrate into a life of Zen practice. Zen practice is applicable and accessible in and as our lives, without exception.

- A habit, such as mala beads or some other wardrobe item, can remind us to engage in Zen practice throughout the day.

- Zen is not in opposition to modern technology. The alarms and alerts that interrupt our attention can also cue us to practice awareness.

- A dedicated practice space can help us access a centered state of mind quickly.

- Kindness and grace toward yourself and others is essential for the Zen path.

CHAPTER 5

ZEN HAPPINESS AT WORK

A morning Zen practice will set you up for a day of engaging in mindful awareness. But just as eating breakfast doesn't mean you can skip lunch, a morning Zen practice doesn't mean you should skip any practices throughout the rest of your day. In this chapter, we'll focus on building a rhythm to keep the practice of Zen going even when your schedule is strewn with distractions, responsibilities, and stress. Allowing Zen to intersect with our busiest of workdays can be challenging, but doing so will yield the awareness that brings the blossoming of happiness into our lives.

Jason: An All Too Typical Day at Work

Jason enjoyed his job and the people he worked with. He was paid well, received reasonable benefits, and didn't have to work weekends. Overall, this job was a good thing. Still, Jason couldn't help but feel a bit unsettled, like he was supposed to be doing more with his life. Throughout this particular morning, he found himself daydreaming about being somewhere else, sometimes just blankly staring at a social media stream on his phone. Realizing the day had gotten on quicker than he'd presumed, Jason turned down a lunch invitation so he could play catch-up with his morning tasks.

An hour or so rolled by, and it was time for an afternoon meeting. He silently bemoaned that this meeting could no doubt have been handled with an email—and even then, the email could have been avoided if the powers that be would have just run the reports that were available at their fingertips. Jason wouldn't exactly say the array of *could have*, *should have*, and *would have* that he frequently bumped into was drudgery. But it wasn't productive, either. Or, more importantly, fulfilling. Moseying into the assigned conference room, Jason stayed as engaged as everyone else while proactively eyeing the clock for an acceptable departing hour to approach.

By the time that early evening had rolled around and it was time to leave the office, Jason was tired. He decided to grab some fast food on the way home, so he could spend the remainder of his night relaxing without the need to cook or deal with the dishes. The next morning would come soon, and not a Saturday morning at that.

ESTABLISHING AN INTENTIONAL RHYTHM OF LIFE

There is little use in establishing parameters for your practice if they extend through only a small portion of the day, or if their rhythm isn't in step with how you attend to the content of your life. The morning practices in chapter 3 are wonderful touch points for establishing a Zen life. But attention must also be paid to establishing touch points throughout your day.

Establishing an intentional daily rhythm strewn with touch points is a somewhat amorphous instruction at first glance. Here are some guidelines to get you started.

Survey your schedule. List the time that you have available for the tasks of a typical workday (or an errand-heavy Saturday, or any other day that's heavily booked). For each task or responsibility, assign a reasonable segment of time to intentionally accomplish it—twenty-, thirty-, or even forty-five-minute segments. Then schedule a break, whether it's a short moment, several minutes, or whatever time's available before switching to a new task or returning to a longer one.

Assign practices to your pauses. Breaks are the perfect time to make contact with your Zen practice during a busy day. Consider how much time you have, and use it for one of the practices described in this book: intentional deep breathing, taking a short but mindful walk or stretch, bringing a mondo phrase or koan to mind, or even cutting through stress-inducing patterns of thought with a clearing mantra.

Stick to the plan. Even for advanced practitioners, the crux of this practice is to formalize a container and rhythm and stick to it. Rather than chalking out a mental estimation of your daily touch points, write your agenda down. Follow the points on the schedule as if they were the bells and drums in a Zen temple, calling you back into mindful awareness of your total experience. (And remember to be compassionate to yourself on days when you miss the call.)

SHAPING OUR THINKING WITH OUR WORDS

In our opening story for this chapter, we found Jason somewhat begrudgingly attending a meeting that "could have" or maybe even "should have" been an email. The reality, however, is that it was not. A meeting had been called, and the only two options for Jason were to attend or not and accept the consequences of either decision. This is a good reminder that an awakened life demarcated with happiness is not to be had in some other distant, far-off, "could have been" reality. It occurs in this very moment, the only true refuge any of us really have access to. We can't go back in time and make a change that will improve our situation or fast-forward to an imagined future when our problems will be solved.

Cognitively reframing our approach to life helps us understand that. One way to do this is by bringing our inner self-talk into accord with the aspirations we have for our Zen path. For this practice, try for a time to eliminate the phrases *could have*, *should have*, and *would have* from your lexicon. Take note when these phrases arise in your thinking or appear on your tongue, and correct them in the moment. Affirm simply what has taken place or what is taking place as the only reality, with language such as "This meeting is happening now." "My kid forgot to take his lunch to school." "I've misplaced my car keys." Invest your mental faculties into the fullness of your actual experience, rather than expending energy on an imagined or even reimagined reality.

ENGAGING THE AVERSE

While proper rest and relaxation are essential components of both a happy and an awakened life, it can be important to examine which specific forms of rest and relaxation we tend to engage in. From the Zen perspective, deriving pleasure, and even rest, from the ordinary processes of life is a characteristic of awakened people. When we apply the sanctifying power of concentrated attention to even the most mundane of activities, we find time and time again that routine tasks and chores can be realized as sacred and pleasurable.

Zen asks us to be profoundly in touch with the ordinary and, beyond being in touch, to be profoundly engaged with it. Try to cultivate that via this practice.

Choose a chore. What daily activities and responsibilities do you find yourself dreading, avoiding, or halfheartedly engaging just to get them done? Washing the dishes? Changing the cat litter? Vacuuming? Pick one to work on.

Engage with it. Dedicate sufficient time each day to mindfully complete the task in question. While performing it, take in the sights, sounds, feelings, and smells (and, where relevant, tastes) of the experiences. Inquire about them. Where is there joy or fulfillment to be found in completing each step of this duty, which might have gone overlooked or unnoticed?

Be persistent. Can't find any pleasure or relaxation in this task? Keep at it, each time performing with more and more intentionality until your resistance to the activity starts to loosen. When the obligation no longer triggers avoidance but feels like an invitation, apply this practice to another ordinary experience.

YOUR WORK KOAN: ZHAOZHOU'S WASH YOUR BOWLS

A young monk once approached Zen Master Zhaozhou and said, "I have just entered the monastery. Please teach me."

Zhaozhou responded, "Have you had breakfast yet?"

"Yes, I have," replied the monk.

"Then," Zhaozhou said, "wash your bowls." At this, the young monk immediately glimpsed awakening.

CONTEMPLATING ACCORD

The sage advice of Master Zhaozhou to the new Zen trainee was that having eaten breakfast, he should wash his bowls. Tending to our responsibilities as they arise, and rooting out the cognitive gaps that lead us to avoid our responsibilities, is a core component of living in accord with reality as it presents itself.

For this practice, ask yourself:

Where do I find myself out of accord with the calls of my daily life? Perhaps not refilling the coffee pot in the office after using it, or stacking dishes in the sink after a meal instead of washing them on the spot?

What story am I telling myself that conflates doing this activity with extra drudgery? Does my narrative about this experience or demand stress me out more than actually performing the task?

Choose one of the tasks you've identified to focus on each day for a week. Simply accomplish the designated task at its naturally indicated time, and while doing so observe your internal commentary. How does your inner dialogue color your experience?

"GO DRINK TEA!"

Tea drinking and tea culture are intimately intertwined with Zen history, mythology, and practice. In fact, in Zen and tea circles, a popular story attributes the first tea plants as springing from the eyelids of the founding master of the Zen tradition (the sage Bodhidharma, whom we met in chapter 1) after he cast them aside in pursuit of a continual investigation of the nature of mind and being in meditation. The implication of this story is that we no longer have to resort to self-mortification in that way the Bodhidharma is said to have done. Riding on the effects of his practice, we can now simply enjoy some tea (caffeinated, if we so choose) to help us remain alert in our practice.

In traditional koan practice done in partnership with an accomplished spiritual teacher, a phrase common to some Zen lineages is "Go drink tea." It's used as a way to express to struggling students that their understanding of a koan, or even a life quandary, is not sufficient. Think of it as an invitation for the student to dismiss themselves and retire to their room, to continue their proactive investigation of the matter at hand.

For this practice, when you're finding yourself weary from the tasks of the day, take five or ten minutes to mindfully prepare a cup of tea. Take in the qualities of the water as it warms your cup and produces steam; take in the fragrance and color created by steeping the tea. Give it sufficient time to steep, striving to perfect the subtle art of not over- or under-concentrating your brew.

As the tea approaches an appropriate temperature, sip it mindfully, aware of all of the sensations its temperature, texture, and flavor elicit. Focusing only on the experience of brewing and drinking the tea, you remain engaged in the practice of intentional awareness but provide yourself some space from any specific task. After your pause for tea practice, you can reengage with renewed vigor.

CONTEMPLATING THE PURSUIT OF ENDLESS PRODUCTIVITY

The crux of this contemplation practice is to examine your own values with regard to work, productivity, and the rationale for seeking practices such as Zen.

Ask yourself:

What led me to look for happiness outside of my present experience?

What factors seem to be inhibiting my realization of well-being?

Do I expect joy to manifest in my life with a mere change of my perspective, or are there outside factors and demands present in my life that also need to change?

If no one were there to judge my words, what would I have to say about the current demands and conditions of my working life?

Practicing Zen to treat our discomfort with the human condition, while perhaps an adequate starting point, is rarely sufficient to produce meaningful change. The happiness and joy that Zen has to offer are not simply found by adding practices and perspectives to your life, but by deconstructing and examining the whole of your life—nothing can be exempt. At the same time, there are few, if any, limits on the diverse array of life expressions and activities that are possible for a Zen practitioner, compared to any other variety of person. Honesty and integrity in the process of holistic examination of your experiences (also called awareness) and therefore accepting the experiences and behaving accordingly (which sometimes demands proactively changing the conditions) are central to every expression of life upholding an integrated, and therefore effective, Zen practice.

DHARMA FOR WORK: A DAY WITHOUT WORK

The Tang dynasty Zen Master Baizhang Huaihai was a particularly esteemed teacher with many disciples. Nonetheless, Baizhang didn't wall himself up in a suite in his monastery complex. Rather, he would work alongside his students each day in the upkeep of the grounds and the smooth running of the monastery operations. As the old master neared his ninetieth year, his students began to fear for Baizhang's health. One morning, the students hid all of the master's tools, hoping to encourage him to slow down. After looking for his tools in vain, however, the old master eventually retired, refusing to eat. "A day without work is a day without food," he famously said. He reiterated the same behavior and speech day in and day out until his students were forced to return his working implements to him. At this, Baizhang once again began to take his daily meals with his fellow monks after resuming his daily work.

MINING EXPECTATIONS

We find in the accounts of Zen Master Baizhang's life no thoughts of retirement, no preoccupation with holidays or vacations, and certainly no accounts of fathoming himself above any task. What a lesson! How often do we find ourselves, by contrast, working toward some far-off day when we'll be able to give up our daily demands and ride out our remaining years on accumulated and deferred bliss?

While it could be easy to look toward Baizhang's example as a demand of constant productivity, the invitation is really about engagement with and the maintenance and integration of the whole of your life experience.

For this exercise, mine your expectations to identify what horizons you may be working toward. Are you awaiting a distant experience that will somehow suddenly bring joy to your life, whether it's an upcoming three-day weekend or a full-blown retirement? Ask yourself:

Are the rewards I'm working toward real potentials or just stories to keep myself motivated?

Why do I need such motivation? What needs to change in my current experience for me to realize my life as worthwhile in the present?

Perhaps an actual change is required—you may be working too many hours or pursuing the wrong profession. But very frequently it's a change in perception and regard that will bring connection to this aspect of your life. In any case, Zen practice is almost always about awareness. The same regard that can manifest this self-inventory as a Zen practice can transform your present experience from a life suspended to a life embodied.

WALKING MEDITATION

Walking meditation can bring great relief to the real pains of spending periods of time in still concentration. Zen does not seek to nurture discomfort; rather, we're always concerned with awareness, acceptance, and accord—responding to reality in meaningful and sensible ways.

In a classical Zen training environment, periods of formal seated meditation are generally interspersed with periods of walking meditation. Walking meditation is a way of extending the processes of seated meditation while paying mind to the real needs of the body, which include movement.

Different schools of Zen may practice a slow, codified motion in walking meditation or alternate between slow walking and near jogging. Other schools, such as that of Zen Master Thich Nhat Hanh, practice a very informal, nature-based form of walking meditation that places emphasis on mindfully taking in the experience of the body's intuitive engagement with reality. That method is perhaps the option best transmitted in book form.

At regular intervals, take up five- or ten-minute walking periods. You can either carry your mental processes with you as you walk or clear your mind by taking in the sights, sounds, and sensations that you encounter. In doing so, pay attention to how your mind responds to stepping out of sedentary contemplation and/or demands that a workday so often places on the body.

THINKING MEDITATION

The reality of the Zen tradition is that it contains a practically infinite array of possible practices. Thinking (a practice perhaps better described as contemplation) has a very important place in Zen practice, so long as it's engaged as the tentative process that it is (contemplation should not undermine your beginner's mind).

Literally anything can be brought into the container of zazen (seated meditation) and be processed as a practice in accord with the principles of Zen. For this practice, choose a case study, a koan, a story, or any contemplative exercise contained in this book—or even a life quandary or raw emotion—and process it during seated meditation.

Always remember that you can bring anything that feels worthy of the fullness of your attention to this practice.

Ask yourself:

How is mindful thinking distinct from mindful experiencing?

What might I be avoiding by enshrining silence and space above my natural cognition?

Can I transmute difficult tasks into accessible experiences by moving them from the ordinary, busied container of life into the emerging container of my meditation practice?

KEY TAKEAWAYS

- You can engage in your Zen practice throughout the day by establishing a rhythm of touch points that call you back into mindful awareness.

- Idioms like *could have* and *should have* distract us from the reality of the present moment, which is where life takes place.

- Mundane tasks that we avoid can become a source of pleasure and relaxation if we examine the reasons we avoid them.

- Zen calls us to examine our whole life, including our values related to our work, productivity, and the rewards that motivate us.

- Thinking is a part of Zen practice as it is a part of our life, and we can use meditation to examine anything worthy of our attention.

CHAPTER 6

ZEN HAPPINESS IN THE EVENING

In this chapter, we'll examine what a typical evening might entail and explore how to process it through a Zen lens, applying the spirit of intentional awareness and practice to your end-of-day agenda. The routine tasks of commuting home, eating dinner, accomplishing evening chores, and finally getting in some rest and relaxation before heading to bed can be cast as a rote, boring, and even tired to-do list. Or, your evening routine can be cultivated as processes of awakening. Read on and we'll seek to nurture a holistic reexamination of a typical evening.

Amari: An All Too Typical Evening

It had already been a long day at work for Amari, made even longer when his supervisor requested a last-minute meeting. The meeting wasn't negative; in fact, it was of little consequence to Amari's day-to-day life, especially to the hours he experienced beyond the confines of his office walls. The later rush hour traffic would be worse than Amari was used to, but it was never good, and he didn't have anything planned in particular for the evening anyway. All in all, the extended workday just meant he was a little closer to the dawning of tomorrow.

Amari's drive home was long, as expected, and while nothing stood out as remarkable, the commute was tiring. Amari had thought about pulling off the interstate to grab a quick dinner, but there was nothing quick about the traffic that evening. Instead, he persisted on his way home. Finally pulling into his garage, Amari parked and sat in silence for a few moments, decompressing before heading up to his apartment. Amari enjoyed his job, but sometimes he wished there was more to life than just working for the weekends.

Opening the door to his apartment, Amari was quickly greeted by his pet cat, who was a little more demanding than affectionate; it was dinnertime, after all. "Just a minute, just a minute," Amari said while hanging up his jacket and keys. "Let me change the laundry first, and then we'll get you your food." After quickly swapping clothes from the washer to the dryer, Amari opened a can of cat food, wishing his own meal prep could be so simple. Before long, Amari got a meal plated for himself and headed to the living room to catch up on the latest episode of his favorite TV series. An hour or so after, having nodded off in his living room chair, Amari roused. He turned off his television, rinsed off his dishes, and headed to bed, now somehow fully awake again.

WORK AS LIFE

As society has evolved, work has become more and more removed from the direct processes of life. For many of us, our daily employment and labor efforts seem disconnected from the immediate satisfaction of any real need and are wrapped up in concerns of salary, health insurance, and retirement plans. Reconnecting our lives to the work we do is essential for overcoming the "working for the weekend" mentality noted in Amari's story.

The practice of reconnecting our lives to our work need not be a grand philosophical experiment. It's a simple matter of investing in the moment fully by connecting our minds and bodies as we perform our tasks and fulfill our responsibilities, instead of separating our thoughts and actions in a disjointed puppet-to-puppeteer relationship.

For this practice, as you make your way through your day, inquire of your mind: Do I find myself daydreaming amid my present tasks? Am I running an internal monologue about being elsewhere or doing anything else than the job at hand?

When your inquiry meets such a state of mind, try this technique. With time, this practice will build a habit of presence and focus.

1. **Connect** with your breath. Pause to intentionally breathe into the fullness of your body.

2. **Feel** the pull of gravity, setting your body into this very moment and space.

3. **Invest** your available agency into the freedom to choose your state of mind. Engage your task at hand, with focus on what you're doing here and now.

4. **Return** to the present moment each time you stray, directing your attention to your breath, your body, and finally your intention.

DRIVING AND THE PRACTICE OF LOVING-KINDNESS

Modern technology makes it easy to commute over distances that would be insurmountable on foot. As our technological capacities have grown, so, too, have our ambitions. Human beings now travel more on a daily basis than at any other point in history. The bumper-to-bumper traffic, technologically distracted drivers, and road rage are enough to test even a Zen Master's patience. But such tests are a real place of practice.

This moment ever defines the whole of our reality. To wish it away is to wish away our very lives. But daily commutes, especially on the way home, are full of moments that try our patience, kindness, and empathy. And therefore, they offer us a place to cultivate those qualities, if we're able to meet such trials with intentionality.

For this practice, commit to wishing loving-kindness to each driver, car, or fellow train or bus passenger who elicits anxiety, frustration, or anger while you're out running errands or heading to work. Contemplate the unknowns of the other person's experience, and articulate—in your mind or out loud, depending on your situation—an aspirational desire for them to be safe, happy, and well. Allow your anger and frustration to dissolve in the light of intentional empathy and genuine concern for the beings with whom you are sharing the road.

CHORES AS PRACTICE

Happiness is to be found only in this moment, not in some far-off existence where we live a life of leisure. But it's easy to become overwhelmed or wistful in facing the small chores and major tasks demanded by our day-to-day home lives. That kind of frustration likely demands a reimagining of our expectations for our lives. Making meaning from our present experience, even when it includes work that doesn't thrill us, is the only way meaning is to be found.

For this practice, begin by making a list of the weekly household responsibilities that are yours to accomplish. Then begin appending them to your formal meditation

The Diamond Sutra Master Deshan was once traveling to southern China to investigate the claims of the Zen monks there, who were said to attain enlightenment through meditation alone, without reliance upon the scriptures. Intending to correct their errant ways, Deshan stopped midway on his journey for some dinner. Greeting the elderly woman who presented as the innkeeper, Deshan explained his current task. The innkeeper responded, "How wonderful! I do have a question for you, being the scholar that you are." Deshan replied, "Ask me anything." The innkeeper said, "The Diamond scripture says that past mind cannot be attained as it is already gone, present mind cannot be attained as it disappears into the past as soon as it is realized, and future mind cannot be attained as it is not yet present. What kind of mind will you then use to eat your dinner?" Deshan stammered but ultimately could not answer.

practice, perhaps just one per day. For example, instead of sitting in meditation for 20 minutes, sit for 10 minutes, and seamlessly carry that meditative intentionality and expansive awareness into the given chore, such as folding the laundry. Do the task with meditative regard, returning to the present moment and present task at hand when your mind wanders. Ask yourself, how does meditation differ between the chair or cushion and the folding table or the dishwasher? If you're finding reasons to draw lines between such activities, keep practicing to see through such arbitrary divisions and enter into the agency of accord.

MEDICINE MEAL

Zen monks traditionally eat only one major meal each day, before noon, and otherwise might enjoy some tea and/or small snacks in the morning and throughout the day. Sustenance taken in the evening was originally allowed in the Buddhist monastic code only under the guise of medicine, and eventually this became known as a "medicine meal." Typically consisting of some type of soup, this final meal of the day is not substantive and therefore avoids causing indigestion or rousing the stomach and digestive system (and thereby the mind) too much before sleep.

For many of us, preparing dinner in the later evening after a long day of work is a considerable task, not only in preparation but even in finding energy to eat and then clean up.

For this practice, consider the possibility of simplifying your evening meals, regarding them as medicine for the maintenance of your body rather than the primary fuel for your life. For example, this may look like preparing a large pot of soup that you can easily portion and reheat throughout the week. A salad that can be easily tossed together and gently digested is another option. How might preparation and simplification alter your experience of your evening, especially after a day of work?

COOKING AS ART

In our modern and ever increasingly busy world, cooking is a task often relegated to the realm of convenience. Restaurants, microwave preparations, and meal delivery services dominate the culinary lives of many modern people. We might see this as an example of life being pushed aside for some estimation of it. We often seek convenience to make space for nothing in particular, hoping that such a void can become an incubator for happiness and meaning.

If work itself can be cast as life, how much easier must it be to imagine cooking as an activity as near to the bone of our humanity as anything? With a bit of practice, or perhaps in casting cooking as a practice, what you might consider a burden or an inconvenience can become an enjoyable and fulfilling activity, integral to your experience of life as a whole.

For this practice, your task is to look at cooking through its classical lens as a functional art. Knowing that you eat with your eyes first, followed by your nose, and finally your mouth, how might you approach the task of cooking your meals as an opportunity for creating art and nurturing life both creatively and aesthetically? If you know some recipes that you'd like to make but have avoided because they seem too time-consuming or complicated, pick one to prepare on a regular basis with intentionality, until it becomes a fulfilling part of your day. If you feel you're lacking in culinary skills, research one easy recipe that you can learn.

EMBRACING SIMPLICITY

Common dietary wisdom notes that we should eat a rainbow; that is, we should vary our diets to include fresh fruits and vegetables featuring a number of different colors, shapes, textures, and flavors. This is an invitation to step outside the rote, overly processed fare common to modern diets and explore the produce aisle or farmers' market, where the roots of food as medicine and as art are to be found in the simplicity of nature's bounty.

For this practice, take a trip to your local grocery store and purchase a selection of fresh, unprocessed ingredients that can be combined or prepared on their own with minimal to do. Perhaps fix a salad, or boil a potato and finish it with a bit of salt and butter. Fresh greens sprinkled with a pinch of salt and drizzled in olive oil with a twist of lemon can make for a bountiful feast when mindfully eaten, allowing the experience of the color, smell, texture, and flavor to be what they are, rather than being dismissed as "just a salad."

The sky is the limit, so long as the crux of the practice remains intact: embracing the simplicity of your ingredients and their preparation, and mindfully engaging them for what they are.

DHARMA FOR THE EVENING: DŌGEN'S EVENING VERSE

Very frequently, the last words spoken each day by practitioners of the Japanese Soto Zen school are invoked in the form of a chanted verse penned by the founder of the school, the great Zen Master Eihei Dōgen. The verse reads as follows: "Let me respectfully remind you that life and death are of supreme importance. Time swiftly passes by and opportunity is lost. Each of us must strive to awaken. Awaken. Take heed. This night your days are diminished by one. Do not squander your life."

Certainly, this verse is a sobering sound to leave on your tongue before entering into the intentional silence of the close of an evening, and yet it rings profoundly true. Every moment of our lives *is* our lives. The question, then, is how do we want to live? It is entirely possible to move through time via a series of increasingly short blips, defined by dis-ease, complaints, and wishing that things could be otherwise. Yet it is also possible to take heed of the wisdom accessible to us, and live with intentionality, awareness, meaning, and the joy that tends to accompany a life of aware accord.

THE PRACTICE OF REST AND RELAXATION

What does it mean to "squander [one's] life?" For Master Dōgen, the answer would likely be simple: to waste your life in the foils of unawareness, leading to suffering. That applies not just to the mundane moments of job and household responsibilities, as we've been discussing, but also to the moments that bring us pleasure and joy. The task in those times and all others is integration: to give equal attention and regard to the whole of our experience, literally manifesting an awakened life.

For this practice, your task is to bring your Zen awareness to the most enjoyable and leisurely moments of your life, when you might otherwise be totally immersed in a given activity. When you're going to the movies, a concert, a sporting event, or some other entertaining distraction, take a moment to connect with your breath and feel the pull of gravity setting you into this time and place. Inquire how your mind is. Are you focused on the here and now?

Attending to rest and relaxation in the same way that we try to transform difficult circumstances into focused "moments of Zen" is a difficult task. This, however, is precisely the stuff integration is forged from.

SANCTIFYING OUR CONCERNS

The end of the day is when many people attempt to wind down, reset, and recharge their batteries. Yet frequently, just when we gain a moment away from the most pressing demands of our day, our minds wander into ruminating on what's left undone, or even toward those matters for which there is nothing to be done. It can be tempting in the beginning stages of Zen practice to use meditation as a way to escape these feelings and manifest some sense of blank bliss. To be clear, this is contrary to the aims and objectives of Zen practice.

Our minds and our minds alone make all things, and our rendered attention is thus the only thing that cleaves sky from earth and heaven from hell. For this practice, your objective is to hold the concerns of the day upon your heart in a gentle regard, seeing them as they are.

When you feel an anxiety or concern calling for your awareness, whether it's looming heavy upon your consciousness or merely lingering in the periphery, don't attempt to banish it or distract yourself. Instead, welcome each matter with your full attention.

Examine each concern in your mind, paying each its due regard. Acknowledge what it is that troubles you about this matter. You can do this as a thinking meditation (page 87) or less formally as you sit, lie, walk, or engage in a mundane task.

Remind yourself that right now, all that can be done today has in fact been accomplished. Examine your mind and feel the troubling issues lessen their longing for visibility as you pay them their due regard.

THE PRACTICE OF SLEEP HYGIENE

Quality sleep is an essential aspect of a quality life. Traditional Zen wisdom asks that we follow the rhythms of the day, getting to sleep at nightfall, and rising with (if not slightly before) the dawn. Tradition even advises that we sleep on our left side to prevent acid reflux, avoid eating too close to bedtime, and even then do so only with light fare. Modern life is often at odds with these simple instructions, though, as varied demands can place fairly immoveable strictures around our schedules. For this practice, your job is to investigate such demands, expressly identify what choices you have regarding your pre-sleep activities, and make any changes needed to obtain adequate nightly rest.

Some general guidelines for good sleep hygiene include having a consistent, set time to go to bed (even on the weekend) and giving yourself enough sleep time to wake up feeling rested (typically this is six to eight hours of sleep). Try establishing a peaceful ritual that starts an hour before bedtime, such as reciting Dōgen's Evening Verse, perhaps appended to an evening meditation and then abiding in silence (with no electronic devices or screens) for the rest of that time. Activities like reading and journaling, with dimmer, warmer lighting than you might use during the day, are well-embraced as part of a sleep hygiene in accord with your Zen practice.

KEY TAKEAWAYS

- Because happiness occurs in the present moment, not some imagined future, Zen encourages us to examine and connect with our whole lives, including our work, household chores, and responsibilities as well as our moments of pleasure and joy.

- Trying moments, like the stress of a daily commute, are an opportunity to cultivate patience, kindness, and empathy.

- Cooking our food and preparing meals are activities close to our humanity. We can and should integrate these activities with our experience of life as a whole, not treat them as if they were inconvenient chores.

- Zen is not a method for avoiding what troubles us. Rather, it encourages us to apply our full attention to our concerns, so we can accept them and act in accord with reality.

CHAPTER 7

ZEN HAPPINESS WHEN HAPPINESS SEEMS IMPOSSIBLE

There is wisdom in the Eastern meditative traditions that advise us to "Practice while you can; you'll need it when you can't." Our daily lives may sometimes be so busy that substantive meditation—or any task not related to the demands of productivity—seems an impossibility. But the time to practice and get a handle on our lives is always this moment. In this chapter, we'll explore ways to put our Zen practice to work when it truly seems impossible, when confronting our immediate experience with intention and attention is difficult to do.

Maria: Zen in Difficult Moments

Maria, a single mother of three young boys, recently lost her job due to downsizing. In a difficult job market, she was quick to accept the first role offered that would pay her bills and provide for her children, even if it meant accepting the ninety-day probationary period. During her first ninety days on the new job, Maria would receive no healthcare benefits and no sick days or other paid time off.

Things were tough for Maria and her family. Her father had recently entered the final phases of a long battle with a terminal illness. Regularly fielding phone calls from her sisters and mother updating her on her father's condition, Maria longed to be with her family. But her new job provided no leeway to do so. Fearing losing her home and not being able to quickly find other adequate employment, Maria hunkered down at work but struggled while tending to her emotions and family relationships as best she could.

Maria had learned to meditate during a corporate retreat day at her former place of employment. Finding that meditation did seem to keep her more focused and calm throughout the day, Maria practiced sitting meditation most mornings. But lately she was having a hard time getting through her twenty-minute sessions. Maria's mind would wander and quickly turn to ruminating on her situation, her family, and, most of all, her feelings of hopelessness through it all. *I just don't know what to do*, thought Maria. *I don't even know what I'm doing right now.* Standing up long before her usual twenty minutes of meditation elapsed, Maria set out to meet the remaining demands of the day.

ESTABLISHING A FIELD
OF CONTEMPLATION

Seated meditation practice is frequently misunderstood. Often cast as an activity intended to merely settle your thoughts or eliminate stress, the discipline of meditation stretches much deeper than this. In Zen, settling your thinking is not a goal unto itself; rather, the stillness and clarity of mind achieved through meditation can, in many ways, be understood as establishing a field of contemplation, a clear desktop upon which work can be accomplished. What is that work? Meditation in general and Zen in particular should not be regarded as merely a tool for outward productivity and efficiency. The "great work of life and death" (as Zen is often termed by adepts) includes such concepts but goes beyond them.

For this practice, after you've established an ongoing meditation practice, be alert for what may seem like the natural apex of your meditation session, perhaps the experience of thoughts and seemingly errant streams of consciousness finding their place in a cohesive whole. Instead of bounding from that moment into your day, pause and abide there.

When you're able to do this consistently, bring in the concerns of your heart and the weights on your interior life and well-being. Examine, possibly deconstruct, and otherwise become intensely familiar with these burdens. The interior work that you're trying accomplish in this practice is that of understanding, making sense where senselessness once stood, and becoming one with your life experiences as an integrated whole.

MOURNING WITH INTENTION

In the liturgical side of the Zen tradition, there are numerous rituals that have been established to help guide adherents of the Zen way through the sometimes murky waters of life with the clarifying powers of intention and attention. Some of the most significant losses that human beings incur in the course of their lives are those of other beloved beings and relationships, often to death but also to other assorted forces and conditions. In the Western world, the implied expectation of mourning these losses is for our grief to be neatly packaged into a singular event and never again publicly revisited (save perhaps in the confines of a grief counselor's office).

In the Zen practice of mourning, especially around death, a loss that someone has incurred is invoked in their daily experience and practice every day for at least forty-nine days, and then again at one hundred days, and again at the one-year mark. And this is the minimal expectation. During such times, you're expected to make offerings (appropriate to the loss or concern) to a small altar or table and meditate in front of it, abiding in this field of contemplation established in your Zen practice and processing your feelings and thoughts.

At the end of each session, an intention is set for the benefits of your practice to be extended to lost loved one(s) amid the mystery of their transition or difficulty. For example, you might say, "May ____ be happy and well," "May they find quick and auspicious rebirth," or "May their journey into the unknown be comfortable, safe, and meaningful," adding, "May the merits of my practice work toward these aims." This practice works to establish acceptance, promote generosity, and root out the seeds of potential trauma related to a loss.

LOOKING BEYOND THE CONVENTION OF DUALITY

The primary philosophical underpinning of the Western world is a supposition of duality: good or bad, on or off, this or that. Dualistic thinking often serves to limit our potential by obscuring our path as nothing but a series of interlinking binary decisions. Zen directly challenges this type of thinking, noting that often seeming opposites can occupy the same space and ultimately exist in a non-negating mutuality.

For this exercise, explore your dualistic thinking by observing your usage of the word *or*. Spend a day or longer taking note of where this word appears in your thoughts and speech. Experiment with swapping *or* for the word *and*. How often does this point to an option or path that you otherwise would have disregarded or considered impossible? How certain are you that a particular statement of *and* can't be accomplished?

For instance, we may say, "I could quit my job, or I can make enough money to survive." This is, in psychological terms, is all-or-nothing thinking. More true, and inviting the fullness of life's potential and experience, would be to say, "I could quit my job and make enough money to survive doing something else."

Conventional thinking is but one way of meeting reality. The unconventional, which can be accessed through your ongoing Zen practice, may meet your needs in any given quandary with more freedom and a better fit than a binary, this-or-that way of thinking.

**YOUR KOAN FOR
DIFFICULT MOMENTS**

Zen Master Ko Bong once asked, "The whole universe is on fire. Through what kind of samadhi can you escape being burned?"

All states of experience, and all people, places, and things, are temporary, like wood being consumed in a fire. All things eventually come to a transformative end. Zen Master Ko Bong reminds us that even when our lives seem to be going without a hiccup, temporality is ever on our tails. Are we aware of it? If aware, are we in acceptance and accord with it? Is there a solution to this? If so, how can it be found?

EXPLORING SAMADHI

The word *samadhi* refers to a particular variety of concentrated meditative absorption wherein time and space—and perhaps even self—seem to fall away to the eternity that underpins every moment. Zen Master Ko Bong's koan posits that there are many types of samadhi, perhaps beyond this generic enveloping experience that we sometimes bump into during our meditation practice. What type of meditative absorption can deliver us through the variegated trials of life unscathed or unscorched?

For this practice, it is important to remember the value of finding a way to transcend the binary—not to avoid duality but to go beyond it. In your meditation, atop your established field of contemplation, bring to mind images of current or previous experiences that felt as though they set your very universe ablaze. Find yourself in these experiences. Inquire of your body what state it was in during or after the calamity. Ask yourself:

Can a state of being burned and a state of being unscathed coexist in the same body?

Can fire itself be burned?

Is it possible to become one with the all-enveloping flames that sometimes befall our experiences?

Attempt to describe this experience to yourself without using words.

INVITING EXPERIENCE

The fundamental essence of Zen practice is concentrated attention, cultivated upon intent. But what is the object of that attention? In times of relative ease, it can be simple to slip into a mode of vegging out during our Zen practice, simply enjoying the relative stillness of meditation for the sake of stillness itself. In times of difficulty, though, such carefree bliss riding often becomes inaccessible. In this way, difficulty comes as a benevolent teacher, correcting our practice by spurring us to examine and act in accord with the reality of our life.

The great Zen Master Kyong Ho once said, "Don't hope for a life without problems. An easy life results in a judgmental and lazy mind." He then went on to invoke the advice of sages of the distant past, who always invited practitioners to "accept the anxieties and difficulties of this life." For this exercise, regard your meditation practice less as a place to zone out and more as a place to tune in. And, ultimately, a place to accept your present reality and act accordingly, with wisdom and grace.

Before beginning a meditation session, ask yourself:

What is compelling me to meditate?

What is chiefly concerning or disrupting to my mind?

When you've identified your concern, instead of seeking to overcome or circumvent it, use your meditation to enter into it. Invite the troubling experience to be with you as you inquire about its structure and components. Become so familiar with this experience or feeling that it dissolves in your concentration and you can navigate it as a neutral observer.

ABIDING IN DISCOMFORT

Throughout the chapters of this book, we've explored the practice of intentional unknowing, of taking refuge in the moment even when it seems to lack the comforts we desire. Unknowing can be a somewhat uncomfortable position, but with Zen we gain familiarity with experiencing it. Concerns for the discomforts of unknowing tend to fade away.

This exercise calls us to look similarly toward the discomfort of difficult moments, whether physical or emotional pain, fatigue, distress, or even generalized anxiety. Instead of seeking to overcome these things or to bring them to some acceptable resolution, this practice asks us to simply see them as they are and let them be without the need to interfere proactively in their genesis, stabilization, or dissolution. In this moment, our job is to simply show up fully and attentively.

Similar to the "Inviting Experience" exercise (page 113), for this practice, enter into meditation with your difficult experiences as your companions. Take note of the discomfort or suffering that you find to be of chief concern to your thinking mind. And instead of seeking to deconstruct, repair, or see through it, your job is to simply be with it, to proactively accompany your discomfort with no other agenda.

So many of our reactions to our life experiences are built on fight-or-flight assumptions. This exercise turns those assumptions on their head and provides a true avenue for taking refuge in this very moment, no matter how difficult.

DHARMA FOR THE DIFFICULT MOMENTS

Zen Master Il Bung was once traveling on a ferry from Jeju Island to the Korean mainland. Midway into the trip, a tempest broke out and quickly threatened to destroy the boat. Perceiving that without quick intervention the ferry would undoubtedly sink, Il Bung looked around at his fellow passengers, most of whom were locked in fervent prayer. Calling out to the passengers, Il Bung held up his monk's knapsack and shouted, "Friends, now is not the time to pray. It is the time to take action! I am a simple monk. Contained in this knapsack are all of my worldly possessions, which I am now willing to toss overboard to lighten our load and save our lives! If I am capable of this, surely so are you. Quickly toss over your bags and boxes in hopes of stabilizing our ferry!"

Heeding his instructions and example, the passengers began tossing over their belongings, and the boat began to stabilize. After the last of the boxes and bags had been thrown overboard, Zen Master Il Bung instructed the assembled passengers, "Now that we have done our part, we can pray to the bodhisattva of compassion to calm our minds." Eventually, the sky cleared, the boat steadied, and all of the passengers and staff safely reached the mainland.

PRAYER AS CONTEMPLATIVE CULTIVATION

Conventionally, prayer is considered to be seeking the ear of some outward power to proactively intervene in the affairs of our lives and shift events toward a preferable direction. While it would be easy to interpret the story of Master Il Bung as relating to the common adage "God helps those who help themselves," there is another interpretation: prayer as a perennial activity of the human heart, throughout time, space, and culture. Under this characterization, prayer need not include hope for a changed outcome or even be directed to a particular addressee (otherworldly or otherwise). Rather, prayer can be a spontaneous function of giving form to our inner experience, so we can approach it with lucidity and awareness.

For this exercise, in either free-form speech or writing, let loose the concerns, desires, hopes, affirmations, and thanks of your heart. You need not direct these to anyone or anything other than this very moment itself, where your experiences arise. Take note, either during this practice in the moment or while reflecting afterward, of how it facilitates catharsis through letting your heart express itself as it is.

SURRENDER AS ACCORD

Human beings are prone to illogical esteem for accumulating experiences and physical possessions. Just as Zen Master Il Bung was quick to set an example in sacrificing all of his worldly belongings, this practice invites us to explore what possessions we might be inappropriately hanging on to. Often the process of meeting any moment fully and acting in accord with it will demand surrender and sacrifice, as Il Bung realized.

Ask yourself: What am I holding on to that's limiting my choices and preventing me from being where and how I need to be in this very moment? A well-paying job that leaves me no time for anything else? A self-image of being perfect that's impossible to sustain? Challenge yourself to give up or surrender one such thing.

CUTTING YOURSELF (AND EVERYONE ELSE) SOME SLACK

The iconoclastic fifteenth-century Japanese Zen Master Ikkyū Sojun once observed that "Yesterday's clarity is today's stupidity." We've noted elsewhere in this book that even the Zen Master's life is but one continuous mistake. How, then, are we, as newer students of the Zen way, to practice? What is the so-called right way to practice and manifest awakening?

Zen Master Taizan Maezumi often invoked an image of enlightenment as a "hazy moon" (in contrast to a "brilliant sun"). That said, the final practice of this brief text is that of forgiveness, which at the end of the day is a child of awareness and acceptance and is in essence then a function of accord.

Stubbing a toe while fumbling through the hazy and dim light of mid-evening is a common enough occurrence. And despite the immediacy of the intense pain it can elicit, it's normally not a trigger of self-blame or self-loathing. Typically, as the pain of your stubbed toe runs its course, so, too, do any errant emotions that came with it, and you continue on your way (perhaps with a lighter step for a time). So, too, must you come to regard the whole of your life as a student of Zen.

Here, the instruction is simple: Forgive yourself, forgive others, and persist in the light and shadow of the hazy moon that will become well-known to your practice.

KEY TAKEAWAYS

- Meditation in the Zen tradition is not a goal unto itself. The stillness and clarity brought on by your meditation practice can be a field of complication on which you can examine and understand the concerns of your heart.

- Zen challenges binary thinking and invites us to replace *or* with *and*.

- Meditation is an opportunity to be with our troubling experiences and accept them as our present reality, so we can then act accordingly with wisdom and grace.

- Prayer can be thought of as giving form and expression to our concerns, desires, hopes, affirmations, and gratitude.

- Enlightenment has been compared to a "hazy moon," and we should forgive ourselves and others for stumbling in its shadows.

CLOSING NOTE

Congratulations! You have now neared the end of your first read of this text. With any luck, you've not only enjoyed a broad view of what comprises and defines the history and praxis of the Zen tradition, but also gained a direct experience or taste of Zen through the pursuit of the exercises and meditations contained within this book. My hope is that you will continue trying out the exercises, putting them to work in your life, and will revisit them frequently.

I cannot stress enough the importance of constancy and return in the practice of Zen. While our efforts may occasionally grant quickly earned glimpses into ways of being that provide much encouragement for the journey ahead, the rubber meets the road only under resistance. When the novelty of your beginning Zen practice wears off, when the forces of familiarity beg your attention elsewhere, and when you finally begin to feel as though there is nothing to see behind the proverbial curtain, keep going. Until you push past that point, you are merely practicing for the sake of practicing. And while that is noble, it's nonetheless not really engaging in the cultivation that has rendered Zen adepts throughout the ages the peace, joy, equanimity, and experience that might be worthy of deeming *happy*.

Life rarely provides us with quick fixes, but for those of us inclined to pay close attention, it does offer clear paths out of our quandaries. Paths that, despite their clarity, are worthwhile or meaningful only when they are traversed. Zen is one such path.

The path of Zen is one of taking refuge in our bare awareness and consciousness itself. It's a path open to all people but one so simple that many are prone to prematurely dismiss it, assuming there is nothing to be had in paying profound attention to the content and processes of their lives. This is the primary hazard to be on the lookout for as you continue in your Zen practice—namely, assuming that you already understand. Be it a Zen practice lasting one day, one year, or one decade, we must keep clear of assuming omniscience and keep to a beginner's mind. This very moment is ever refreshing, always new, and is in fact eternity itself.

In returning to the path each time we stray, we find that the path doesn't so much dissolve as expand, encompassing the whole of our reality with the realization that the sacred now, in its fullness, is ever and always enough. Here, in this enough-ness, can we finally abandon concerns for clarity and stupidity, for wisdom and naivety, and even for happiness itself. Life and happiness come to take care of themselves, should we let them. So please, above all else, pay attention and persist.

RESOURCES

Zen Primers

The following texts are, to this author's knowledge and taste, among the most comprehensive and accessible introductions to the Zen tradition available on the market, with each representing a classic of the emerging movement of Zen in the Western world and English language.

Seung Sahn's text offers a comprehensive, practitioner-oriented examination of the major movements, schools, and scriptures of the wider Buddhist tradition, which culminated in the birth and refinement of the Zen school of our contemporary epoch.

Thien An Thich's text is a collection of classical practices found within the Zen school generally without sectarian focus, inviting Zen students into the practice of Zen's philosophies, rather than merely presenting them for high-level consideration.

Finally, Shunryu Suzuki's text represents a primer in Zen thought, as something of a stream-of-conscious record of one of the great masters of the twentieth century. The text's meaning and content evolve with a practitioner's evolution in the practice, even over decades.

Sahn, Seung. *The Compass of Zen (Shambhala Dragon Editions)*. Edited by Hyon Gak. Boston: Shambhala Publications, 1997.

Suzuki, Shunryu. *Zen Mind, Beginner's Mind: Informal Talks on Zen Meditation and Practice*. New York: Weatherhill, 1970.

Thich, Thien An. *Zen Philosophy, Zen Practice*. Berkeley: Dharma Publishing, 1975.

Collections of Koans, Verses, and Parables

The following titles represent a sampling of the Zen spirit as found in its sacred texts, such as with Zenkei Shibayama's and Thomas Cleary's respective presentations of the *Gateless Barrier* and *Blue Cliff Record* koan collections. Murphy's book brings the ancient koan anthologies to life in the modern world, with a variety of teaching stories and records of encounters with modern-day masters in contemporary situations. Finally, Mitchell's translation of the Daoist classic *Tao Te Ching* gives a Zen-informed reading of one of the seminal wisdom texts of the world's religions, which is clearly at the beating heart of the Zen tradition.

Cleary, Thomas. *Secrets of the Blue Cliff Record: Zen Comments by Hakuin and Tenkei*. Boston: Shambhala Publications, 2000.

Murphy, Sean. *One Bird, One Stone: 108 American Zen Stories*. New York: Renaissance Books, 2002.

Shibayama, Zenkei. *Gateless Barrier: Zen Comments on the Mumonkan*. Translated by Sumiko Kudo. Boston: Shambhala Publications, 2000.

Tzu, Lao. *Tao Te Ching: A New English Version*. Translated by Stephen Mitchell. New York: Harper Perennial Modern Classics, 2006.

Practitioner Biographies

The following titles comprise two sets of biographies of two Western women (the Reverends Jiyu-Kennett Roshi and Gesshin Greenwood) and two men (the Reverends James Ford Roshi and Dennis Kelly Roshi), shining light onto what a life of Zen training might look like in the twentieth and twenty-first centuries, in both Asia and America. These texts are certain to enthrall, inspire, and educate dedicated Zenists and topical explorers alike.

Ford, James Ishmael. *If You're Lucky, Your Heart Will Break: Field Notes from a Zen Life*. Somerville, MA: Wisdom Publications, 2012.

Greenwood, Gesshin Claire. *Bow First, Ask Questions Later: Ordination, Love, and Monastic Zen in Japan*. Somerville, MA: Wisdom Publications, 2018.

Jiyu-Kennett, P. T. N. H. *The Wild White Goose: The Diary of a Female Zen Priest*. 2nd ed. Mount Shasta, CA: Shasta Abbey, 2002.

Martin-Smith, Keith. *A Heart Blown Open: The Life and Practice of Zen Master Jun Po Denis Kelly Roshi.* Perception Press, 2019.

Other

DeSteno's text takes a psychological and general approach to religious traditions and seeks to give light to the science behind many of the practice forms common to Zen and most of the world's great religious traditions.

DeSteno, David. *How God Works: The Science behind the Benefits of Religion.* New York: Simon & Schuster, 2021.

REFERENCES

Cleary, Thomas. *Secrets of the Blue Cliff Record: Zen Comments by Hakuin and Tenkei*. Boston: Shambhala Publications, 2000.

"Happiness." *Merriam-Webster.com*. Accessed December 10, 2021. Merriam-Webster.com/dictionary/happiness.

Seung, Sahn. *The Compass of Zen (Shambhala Dragon Editions)*. Edited by Hyon Gak. Boston: Shambhala Publications, 1997.

Shibayama, Zenkei. *Gateless Barrier: Zen Comments on the Mumonkan*. Translated by Sumiko Kudo. Boston: Shambhala Publications, 2000.

Suzuki, Shunryu. *Zen Mind, Beginner's Mind: Informal Talks on Zen Meditation and Practice*. Weatherhill, 1970.

Treace, Bonnie Myotai. *Zen Meditation for Beginners: A Practical Guide to Inner Calm*. Emeryville, CA: Rockridge Press, 2020.

INDEX